WEST OF SUEZ

WEST OF SUEZ

A PLAY BY JOHN OSBORNE

FABER & FABER

First published in 1971 by
Faber & Faber
3 Queen Square, London WC1
Printed in England by
Latimer Trend & Co Ltd Plymouth
ISBN 0 571 09877 0 (paper-covered edition)
ISBN 0 571 09876 2 (cloth)
© 1971 by John Osborne   All rights reserved

TO J.R.B. AND G.T.

First performed at the Royal Court Theatre on 17th August 1971 with the following cast:

WYATT GILLMAN	RALPH RICHARDSON
FREDERICA	JILL BENNETT
ROBIN	PATRICIA LAWRENCE
EVANGIE	SHEILA BALLANTINE
MARY	PENELOPE WILTON
EDWARD	GEOFFREY PALMER
ROBERT	FRANK WYLIE
PATRICK	WILLOUGHBY GRAY
CHRISTOPHER	NIGEL HAWTHORNE
ALASTAIR	ANTHONY GARDNER
OWEN LAMB	NICHOLAS SELBY
HARRY	PETER CARLISLE
MRS. JAMES	SHEILA BURRELL
LEROI	RAUL NEUNIE
MR. DEKKER	JOHN BLOOMFIELD
MRS. DEKKER	BESSIE LOVE
JED	JEFFREY SHANKLEY
ISLANDER	LEON BERTON
ISLANDER	MONTGOMERY MATTHEW

Directed by Anthony Page
Designed by John Gunter
Lighting by Andy Phillips

CHARACTERS

★

WYATT GILLMAN	A WRITER
FREDERICA	
ROBIN	
EVANGIE	WYATT'S DAUGHTERS
MARY	
EDWARD	FREDERICA'S HUSBAND (a pathologist)
ROBERT	MARY'S HUSBAND (a teacher)
PATRICK	A RETIRED BRIGADIER
CHRISTOPHER	SECRETARY TO WYATT
ALASTAIR	A HAIRDRESSER
OWEN LAMB	A WRITER
HARRY	
MRS. JAMES	AN INTERVIEWER FROM THE LOCAL NEWSPAPER
LEROI	ROBIN AND THE BRIGADIER'S SERVANT
MR. DEKKER	AMERICAN TOURIST
MRS. DEKKER	AMERICAN TOURIST
JED	AMERICAN TOURIST
TWO ISLANDERS	

ACT ONE

*The loggia of a trim, attractive villa on a sub-
tropical island, neither Africa nor Europe, but
some of both, also less than both. Startling shrubs
and trees. Bright, stippled patches, cold, dark
places, a whisper of ocean and still heat. Chairs
reclining in and out of the sun.* FREDERICA *and*
EDWARD, *her husband, are sitting beneath a trailing
vine. She is just in the sun, her eyes closed, he in the
shade, reading a newspaper. Presently, a brown-
ish-coloured servant in a white jacket,* LEROI, *comes
over to the table beside them and laboriously puts
down a glass of iced orange juice and a long exotic-
looking drink in a taller glass.*

EDWARD: Thank you. That's fine.
              (LEROI *stares at the glass, hesitates.*)
              Fine. Thanks. (*To* FREDERICA) Sure you won't
              have a proper drink?
FREDERICA: Sure. Alcohol and me before lunchtime in this
              climate just don't go.
              (LEROI *goes.*)
              It does something to women, anyway.
EDWARD: Well, there are misfortunes all sides. Nothing
              else, thanks, Leroi.
FREDERICA: He's gone. Not that he'd hear you.
EDWARD: They really do stand and stare.
FREDERICA: They're not waiters for nothing.
EDWARD: Yes. A sort of ethnic group. While they last.
FREDERICA: We *last*, you mean. It's an odd mixture.

EDWARD:	What?
FREDERICA:	Them. Lethargy and hysteria.
EDWARD:	Oh yes. I've noticed. Perhaps it's being a small island.
FREDERICA:	Brutality and sentimentality.
EDWARD:	Perched between one civilization and the next.
FREDERICA:	Craven but pleased with themselves.
EDWARD:	Listen to those birds.
FREDERICA:	They're too pleased with themselves as well.
EDWARD:	Jolly pretty.
FREDERICA:	Not pretty enough. Like those same old native songs they sing every night. And those dreadful instruments. One of the worst things about England.
EDWARD:	What?
FREDERICA:	Bloody birds. Making a din, first thing you hear.
EDWARD:	Only in the country.
FREDERICA:	No, in London as well. Wake me up every day.
EDWARD:	Don't know what we can do about your sleep.
FREDERICA:	Neither do I.
EDWARD:	Still, better than aeroplanes.
FREDERICA:	Um?
EDWARD:	Birds.
FREDERICA:	Oh. Don't see why. I rather like the sound of aeroplanes. At least they're useful. I thought I'd be all right, marrying a doctor.
EDWARD:	All right for what?
FREDERICA:	Oh, everything. Getting to sleep, I suppose.
EDWARD:	Well, I have *tried*.
FREDERICA:	Oh, you all *try*.
EDWARD:	Thanks a hump.
FREDERICA:	I think doctors are an oddly narrow lot on the whole.
EDWARD:	We try not to give rise to incident.
FREDERICA:	Indeed. Don't forget to dispense negatives. Like

Civil Servants. I didn't used to think so.

EDWARD: I suppose you're really a bit of a whore about medicine.

FREDERICA: Oh, I'll try anything once.

EDWARD: But not necessarily twice.

FREDERICA: Doctors are to be *used*.

EDWARD: Like bookmakers.

FREDERICA: Right. They never lose . . .

EDWARD: We all lose.

FREDERICA: Some sooner and quicker.

EDWARD: No. That's how we start out.

FREDERICA: Or faster and funnier.

EDWARD: No. Not very funny.

FREDERICA: Oh, I think so. Don't you really?

EDWARD: No.

FREDERICA: I do. What's dull is people who don't know they've lost already. Like Leroi.

EDWARD: That's a misnomer, I must say.

FREDERICA: They're all misnomers, if you ask me. Mr. and Miss Nomers . . .

EDWARD: I think you concern yourself a bit too much about sleeping.

FREDERICA: You mean I shouldn't?

EDWARD: No. But——

FREDERICA: But what?

EDWARD: You know what I was going to say, so what's the point?

FREDERICA: Perhaps you might surprise me for once.

EDWARD: I doubt it.

FREDERICA: Now *you* sound pleased.

EDWARD: You shouldn't incite me to repeat myself.

FREDERICA: Then why rise to it?

EDWARD: Why lay it?

FREDERICA: No quarry, no bait, I suppose is that answer.

EDWARD: It's a habit people have when they've lived at

13

close quarters for long. People *can* live without too——

FREDERICA: Much sleep. Like you?

EDWARD: It can be acquired. Or not.

FREDERICA: What do you do instead?

EDWARD: Keep awake?

FREDERICA: And the options?

EDWARD: What you fancy.

FREDERICA: And if there's nothing you fancy?

EDWARD: Do nothing and don't panic.

FREDERICA: Keep the patient in a warm blanket, if possible, with hot sweet tea.

EDWARD: That sort of thing.

FREDERICA: Thanks, doctor. I don't know what we'd do without your medical skill.

EDWARD: Survive, in most cases. . . . Sure you won't have something stronger than that?

FREDERICA: Quite sure. What's that flowery thing you've got?

EDWARD: Rum with local flora and fauna.

FREDERICA: Looks disgusting.

EDWARD: It does. Bit cloying and pleased with itself, as you'd say. But quite pleasant. Try a bit.

FREDERICA: No thanks. I've had all the hangovers I want in this place.

EDWARD: Good for boredom.

FREDERICA: You mean I'm bored?

EDWARD: Didn't occur to me. . . . Did you mean what you just said?

FREDERICA: What? About birds?

EDWARD: Well, that too . . .

FREDERICA: Why shouldn't I mean it? I didn't realize you were such a bird lover. If one can still use it in the feathered sense.

EDWARD: And about losing . . .

FREDERICA: You think I lie?

14

EDWARD: No. Only that——

FREDERICA: What? Only?

EDWARD: The ones who make an ethic out of truthfulness
             do incline to rhetoric.

FREDERICA: You mean I put on a show of feelings I don't
             have?

EDWARD: Not necessarily.

FREDERICA: Then what?

EDWARD: I don't know.

FREDERICA: Then why say it?

EDWARD: Say what?

FREDERICA: What you said.

EDWARD: I don't remember.

FREDERICA: Then you should. You've a trained, scientific
             mind.

EDWARD: Only in a very narrow discipline.

FREDERICA: I don't think you could call pathology narrow.
             Somewhat inhuman and requiring a detachment
             that's almost unscientific. *If* that's what I mean.

EDWARD: You see. It *is* difficult. So let's not pursue it,
             shall we?

FREDERICA: "Let's not pursue it, shall we?" If you really do
             think you've got the gift of scientific lucidity,
             you'd better brush up on your English a bit.

EDWARD: Blood and shit.

FREDERICA: A blood and shit man.

EDWARD: That's all I need to look at all day, just as——

FREDERICA: I always remind you.

EDWARD: As you do. Which isn't quite necessary as I'm
             only too conscious of it.

FREDERICA: Then why should I remind you of it?

EDWARD: Only you and God knows. You wouldn't, or
             what's even more likely, couldn't, and I don't
             see much chance of God revealing any of his
             prime moves or divine intention.

FREDERICA: Oh, that was quite good . . .

EDWARD: What was?

FREDERICA: That sentence. It had almost a syntactical swing about it.

EDWARD: But not quite.

FREDERICA: Not bad though.

EDWARD: "Syntactical" 's a pretty poor word to flash at anyone.

FREDERICA: Don't spar with me.

EDWARD: I wouldn't dream of it. I haven't the equipment.

FREDERICA: You haven't.

EDWARD: Or inclination.

FREDERICA: Or energy.

EDWARD: Or stamina.

FREDERICA: Or interest.

EDWARD: That either.

FREDERICA: Then why are you here then?

EDWARD: To have a refreshing, enhancing holiday with my wife.

FREDERICA: You don't really like holidays . . .

EDWARD: My sister-in-law's very pleasant villa with their family and friends.

FREDERICA: Or anything else for that matter.

EDWARD: That's right, actually. Sometimes, your open-ended tongue does tip over a real, palpable truth.

FREDERICA: What *are* you interested in?

EDWARD: I told you: blood and shit.

FREDERICA: Something passive.

EDWARD: The specimens I see are very active indeed.

FREDERICA: You should have married someone like Robin.

EDWARD: Like looking down a volcano sometimes. I think I *have* said I think your sister's quite a nice girl but a trifle more dull with it than I'd have thought necessary.

FREDERICA:	Or Evangeline.
EDWARD:	I thought we——
FREDERICA:	Oh yes, you don't like intellectual women.
EDWARD:	It's the truth.
FREDERICA:	So you keep saying.
EDWARD:	No. So you keep asking. Like most men——
FREDERICA:	Of your background, yes——
EDWARD:	I'm dim and dismal enough to find them intimidating.
FREDERICA:	Intimidating? She's pathetic.
EDWARD:	Not specially attractive I'd have thought, but pathetic no, no more than the rest of us. She's got a thumping success of a career, which is what she says all the time is the only really important thing.
FREDERICA:	You mean it isn't?
EDWARD:	To her it is, so she always tells me whenever I talk to her. I can't believe it's just a common . . . or a gambit or whatever. Being a man, as you say, I've never had to define myself about a career. Just a plain old blood and shit man who does it because it's the one skill he's managed to more or less master and the one he can pay the bills with in any sort of comfort . . .
FREDERICA:	I think you're taken in by her.
EDWARD:	I've always been prone to being taken in, as easily as a pussy cat's laundry.
FREDERICA:	Now you're straining.
EDWARD:	She's certainly no more pathetic than Robin.
FREDERICA:	What do you mean?
EDWARD:	You know quite well what I mean. You've said it often enough yourself.
FREDERICA:	She's *my* sister.
EDWARD:	Running off with the old Brigadier.
FREDERICA:	I thought you said you liked him?

EDWARD:	I do. I certainly don't hold him in the contempt you do.
FREDERICA:	He's too old and doddery by half.
EDWARD:	He'll outlast *her*.
FREDERICA:	While the money holds out.
EDWARD:	But then contempt comes easily to you.
FREDERICA:	I keep most of it for myself.
EDWARD:	Then try spreading the load or turning down the pressure or something.
FREDERICA:	I happen to like high standards, starting with number one.
EDWARD:	Perhaps you should have a go at observing them, whatever they are. Like try charity for a bit. Give *that* a whirl.
FREDERICA:	Don't start giving me St. Paul. That's the prig's first.
EDWARD:	You think you *don't* sound priggish?
FREDERICA:	The woman was made for the man, not the man for the woman or whatever it is.
EDWARD:	If only he'd pop in on one of his journeys now——
FREDERICA:	He'd be made welcome. I'm sure. Visiting fireman.
EDWARD:	Well, he *did* say better to marry than to burn. Perhaps he meant it the other way round. Bad translation. Sort of Hebraic inversion. . . . Anyway, I think the Brigadier's quite happy.
FREDERICA:	So he should be.
EDWARD:	Why should he be? Because he's a nice simple old stick and he's happy pottering around all day building his little walls and grottoes and making his dreadful old wine for a bob a gallon?
FREDERICA:	And drinking it. . . . He'll not divorce that wife.
EDWARD:	It doesn't seem as if he's able to.
FREDERICA:	Doesn't want to.

EDWARD:	And he's got his children . . .
FREDERICA:	Oh, don't. He's so sentimental about them. They're both six feet five and about thirty and doing better than the old man. I can't understand how he ever held down while he was in the Army.
EDWARD:	The Army's never been short on either sentiment or incompetence. And quite rightly. Anyway, Robin's not exactly a chicken, and even if she is, she's not my idea of the prize of the battery.
FREDERICA:	You accept her hospitality.
EDWARD:	I do. And the fact that I'm not enjoying it too well is no fault of hers.
FREDERICA:	You mean it's mine?
EDWARD:	No, it isn't, Frederica. It's mine. We can't be——
FREDERICA:	Responsible for others.
EDWARD:	Well, I believe it.
FREDERICA:	So you always say.
EDWARD:	Yes. As I always say. It's my responsibility if I am tired, unspontaneous or pretty insubstantial . . .
FREDERICA:	You're sounding pleased again.
EDWARD:	Or *seeming* pleased with myself, which I only wish were sometimes true even.
FREDERICA:	Come.
EDWARD:	If I am unhappy, it is my own responsibility.
FREDERICA:	*Are* you?
EDWARD:	Responsible?
FREDERICA:	Unhappy?
EDWARD:	Fair to Middling to occasional Full Speed Ahead.
FREDERICA:	Thanks.
EDWARD:	I thank myself.

FREDERICA:	You should. Be generous.
EDWARD:	I try to be.
FREDERICA:	To yourself?
EDWARD:	I try not to give myself *too* hard a time . . .
FREDERICA:	It's the others.
EDWARD:	Others what?
FREDERICA:	Give you a hard time?
EDWARD:	No. That would be a delusion.
FREDERICA:	You're not being very clear.
EDWARD:	That's because I'm not what I appear to be.
FREDERICA:	And what are you?
EDWARD:	A middle-aged blood and shit man trying to mop up a bit of sunshine and eat, drink and swim too much, at least not in that order . . .
FREDERICA:	I wouldn't like you to test *my* blood.
EDWARD:	Well I've sampled enough of the other.
FREDERICA:	Shit, you mean. Ah!
EDWARD:	I'm sure your blood is just as lively. . . Well, here's to the Brigadier *and* his wife.
FREDERICA:	You wouldn't say that if they were out there.
EDWARD:	I see no reason to be ungrateful or unkind.
FREDERICA:	What *is* your reason then?
EDWARD:	And to his children, all six foot five of 'em. Perhaps they'll jolly him along when he's tired of it all.
FREDERICA:	Of Robin?
EDWARD:	No. Just tired. She's past that, anyway.
FREDERICA:	You mean *he* is.
EDWARD:	I'd say he was quite a good old rattler. Gets his oats twice a day like an old horse on his holidays.
FREDERICA:	If he can get it up, more likely. Anyway, why should she want to have a child by him even if he could?
EDWARD:	Or *she* could.
FREDERICA:	And what makes you think she couldn't?

EDWARD: Well, she hasn't and she *was* married before for twenty years or whatever.

FREDERICA: So?

EDWARD: So.

FREDERICA: People are capable of making a clear decision about these things.

EDWARD: Like us.

FREDERICA: Like me is what you meant.

EDWARD: Whatever I meant, it turned out you were quite right. And if I ever thought different, I can see how wrong I was . . .

FREDERICA: How much do you really hate me?

EDWARD: I don't know the answer to that one.

FREDERICA: Why not? You're an intelligent man.

EDWARD: You're an intelligent woman.

FREDERICA: You don't think so.

EDWARD: So you say. And as your father would say, I think that is really an opinion posing as a question.

FREDERICA: You disapprove of his going on the telly all the time, don't you?

EDWARD: And *you* certainly can't reply to a question that expresses its own hatred——

FREDERICA: Don't *you*?

EDWARD: I don't disapprove any more than I do of the Brigadier and his wine-making, as long as I don't have to drink it too much.

FREDERICA: You don't though. And how can you compare the Brigadier with my father?

EDWARD: I wasn't and you know it . . .

FREDERICA: What is it that's so fascinating in the newspaper?

EDWARD: The Brigadier is retired and not particularly distinguished even though he's my host and I like him and your father is a busy working writer and very distinguished indeed. All of which is quite different and a waste of my breath and your ears, except they don't function too well.

FREDERICA: They function all right.

EDWARD: It's because I respect what he's done.

FREDERICA: Ah, past tense.

EDWARD: And will quite inevitably do.

FREDERICA: I thought you didn't go much on literature.

EDWARD: I don't. There's enough trouble . . .

FREDERICA: As it is.

EDWARD: Exactly. But looking up occasionally from my smears and slides, I do think someone who is as distinguished and been such a figure, yes, been, is, will still be, continue to be, in nearly all our lives or Western Europe's or at least a few schools and universities and weekly periodicals and newspapers, shouldn't have to clown about doing interviews and literary quiz games and being a fireside character or sage or whatever he is to people, which I've no idea what that is and don't care and neither will they for different reasons and in five minutes either before a new series or after the next programme even. Even . . .

FREDERICA: I don't understand that sentence.

EDWARD: Nor me. But there was some bacteria jumping about in there if you can be bothered and we neither of us can . . .

FREDERICA: You were saying?

EDWARD: I just hope he gets paid all he can get and gets some innocent pleasure out of it, which he's entitled to without censorious philistines like me over-reacting to . . . As for this paper, I quite agree with you that it's pretty deadly——

FREDERICA: Do you think you're getting your sense of humour back again?

22

EDWARD:	As usual . . . I never lost it. It was taken from me by force.
FREDERICA:	By me?
EDWARD:	No. By the mysterious, satanic little creatures that even sober English ladies, Colonels' ladies, residents and missionaries' ladies used to occasionally spot after day-long tennis parties in the dusk of forgotten . . . colonial days.
FREDERICA:	No. Not forgotten.
EDWARD:	No, remembered in white and pink Georgian buildings . . . and the reef piloted through by Nelson himself, and the harbour where the American tourists throw their litter and cartons and beer cans and coke, on the way to the gift shops with their tour guides, and "hello folks", the package smiles and surliness and black feeling all round, all, all of a dimness . . .
FREDERICA:	This place really has got you down.
EDWARD:	No it hasn't. And the reason I read the paper is because the Brigadier goes into town and gets it specially for me every morning.
FREDERICA:	That's his excuse.
EDWARD:	He can't afford it.
FREDERICA:	You mean Robin can't.
EDWARD:	And I know that he'll want to talk about it page by page from the Home news to the leader and letters, to the racing at Catterick and the obituaries and Court Circular.
FREDERICA:	Fascinating.
EDWARD:	Not at all fascinating. But probably as much or as more as he gets from Robin . . .
FREDERICA:	Why do you have to knock my sisters?
EDWARD:	I don't. As you know. You know better than I do.
FREDERICA:	Come on.

23

EDWARD:	What?
FREDERICA:	Please.
EDWARD:	Please come on? Come on what?
FREDERICA:	Be friends.
EDWARD:	We *are* friends.
FREDERICA:	Married—friends.
EDWARD:	Yes. Married—friends . . .
FREDERICA:	You are having a good time, aren't you?
EDWARD:	Yes. Are you?
FREDERICA:	Sure. Can I have some of your drink?
EDWARD:	I'll call Leroi.
FREDERICA:	No. I'll have a sip of yours.
EDWARD:	I'll get another. Leroi!
FREDERICA:	What have I done now?
EDWARD:	Leroi! Come on, you sullen, charmless, un-beautiful, black bastard.
FREDERICA:	Don't get one for *me*.
	(LEROI *ambles in*.)
EDWARD:	Are you sure? Well, I will, anyway. Another one please, Leroi.
	(LEROI *leaves into the cool of the house*.)
	Sorry to be a bother!
FREDERICA:	I wonder what it was like then, when Nelson or Hood or poor old Admiral Byng used to drop in.
EDWARD:	Rather pleasant after being aboard those ships I should think.
FREDERICA:	Would you like to go back?
EDWARD:	Where?
FREDERICA:	Home.
EDWARD:	What for?
FREDERICA:	You're restless.
EDWARD:	One thing I'm not ever is restless, at home or abroad . . . He said, trying to sound as pleased with himself as possible.

FREDERICA:	We're all right, aren't we?
EDWARD:	Fine. All right . . .
FREDERICA:	You don't sound sure.
EDWARD:	Neither do you. But I take your word for it . . .
FREDERICA:	Do you?
EDWARD:	I did just say so . . .
FREDERICA:	Do you think Robin and the Brigadier *will* have any children?
EDWARD:	If they can and want to. Why don't you ask her?
FREDERICA:	I don't like to.
EDWARD:	Would you like *me* to?
FREDERICA:	No. It's too personal.
EDWARD:	Indeed.
FREDERICA:	Private.

(LEROI *comes in and they watch him go through the slow business of putting the drink on the table. He goes.*)

Why do you get cross when I ask questions?

EDWARD:	I don't. Only when you expect answers.
FREDERICA:	Friends?

(*She puts out her hand to him.*)

EDWARD:	Friends.
FREDERICA:	I *did* put out my hand.
EDWARD:	Yes. I know. *First.*
FREDERICA:	Don't say anything . . . I try to be detached.
EDWARD:	Why not? If it makes you feel more real?
FREDERICA:	Real. What's *that*, for God's sake?
EDWARD:	You can produce effects in *real* people. Including me, even. As if you *were* them. Or me.
FREDERICA:	I'm afraid I don't understand that. And I shouldn't think you can.
EDWARD:	No. Sometimes I don't feel I can understand a word of anything anyone says to me. As if they were as unclear as I am . . .
FREDERICA:	Too abstract for me.

EDWARD: If you're wayward.

FREDERICA: *Way*ward?

EDWARD: Oh, or impossible or just dotty enough, you escape every, any coherence or intent that might be in the way . . .

FREDERICA: What'll we do today? Swim before lunch?

EDWARD: Don't think *I* will.

FREDERICA: Do you good.

EDWARD: I know. I've put on weight.

FREDERICA: You have.

EDWARD: Robin's cooking.

FREDERICA: Well I think *I'll* go.

EDWARD: I'll come down with you . . .

FREDERICA: Are you sure you wouldn't rather go home?

EDWARD: Sure.

FREDERICA: You wouldn't like to get back to your work?

EDWARD: No. I don't find work so irresistible.

FREDERICA: That's because you're lucky. You know it's there, waiting for you.

EDWARD: There are equally attractive alternatives to work.

FREDERICA: Like?

EDWARD: Idleness, for one. You can always make a choice.

FREDERICA: Not all of us. It's *behind* us.

EDWARD: Can we leave that one alone for a bit.

FREDERICA: Of course . . . I'll get changed. I can't bear abstractions. Sort of labour-saving devices.

EDWARD: *That* sounds like an abstraction.

FREDERICA: Does it? Well, I'll go for the concrete any time.

EDWARD: That can be just as evasive. Don't ask me what I mean.

FREDERICA: I wasn't going to. I've given all that up . . .

EDWARD: Just as well.

FREDERICA: Um?

EDWARD: I think I'll have a quick dip after all.

(*Enter* MARY, FREDERICA's *youngest sister. Her*

26

husband, ROBERT *with her. Both about mid-thirty.*)

FREDERICA:	Where have you been?
MARY:	Just for a walk, keeping away from the tourists from the cruise ship.
FREDERICA:	Not another lot!
MARY:	I think these are only here for the day. We went along the beach.
EDWARD:	Oh, you hardly ever see them there. They don't like the idea of walking.
FREDERICA:	Don't think they *can*, you mean.
ROBERT:	Few little Nips popping away with cameras and an odd Kraut or two, bellowing at their Fraus.
EDWARD:	Didn't you notice the little fleet of old cartons and coke bottles coming round this way? You can see it from here even. Regular armada out there.
ROBERT:	Also, we thought we'd nip off early so that we didn't have to say goodbye to the Brigadier's mama.
FREDERICA:	She has gone, I hope?
MARY:	Unless the plane's crashed.
FREDERICA:	As long as she's *on* it, that's fine.
MARY:	Robin went with them, to see her off. And the Brigadier's getting the papers and a few other things.
FREDERICA:	We stayed in bed till we thought she'd gone . . .
EDWARD:	Well, the Brigadier seems quite fond of her.
FREDERICA:	He doesn't have to put up with her like the rest of us. He's too busy with his vines or in his workshop making some object. Anyway, I don't think you should call him "Brigadier".
EDWARD:	Well, he is, isn't he?
FREDERICA:	I suppose he is, though I've got my doubts about it. But people don't call you "doctor". Besides you're the only one who calls him it to his face.
EDWARD:	Why not?

FREDERICA:	Because it sounds as if you're sending him up.
EDWARD:	I don't mean to.
FREDERICA:	Maybe.
MARY:	I think you're all a bit mean about his mother. She's not that bad. And she *is* quite old.
FREDERICA:	That is no mitigation any more than youth. She's a crabbed old rat bag. If I'd have known she'd be here I don't suppose I'd have come. Damn it, one of the reasons we came out here was to get away from having to have Edward's mother another Christmas.
MARY:	*And* see Robin and everyone.
FREDERICA:	Sure. But I tell you, I'd have got on the nearest dog-sled to the South Pole to get away from one more Christmas with that old gangster. Complaining, and wailing and scheming, impossible to please. Like having an incontinent, superannuated Mafia in your sitting room all day. Even Edward can't stand her, though he never tells her to her face and he really—and he really —hates her more than I do.
ROBERT:	Men's mums *are* usually worse.
FREDERICA:	The Christmas before I nearly went into the London Clinic afterwards for the rest of the year. Actually, I'll say this, which isn't much, for the Brigadier's mama—she's got a bit more class than Edward's, even if she does pretend she's not deaf. At least, she doesn't look as if she's had the curse every day for the past sixty-five years.
ROBERT:	She's got chronic menstruation, Never laughs, never smiles, Mine's a dismal occupation, Cracking ice for Grandma's piles.
EDWARD:	Oh, *I* remember that.

FREDERICA:	Men——
EDWARD:	What's the verse after that?
ROBERT:	Even now the baby's started,
	Having epileptic fits;
	Every time it coughs it farts,
	Every time it farts it shits.
FREDERICA:	If it's grubby-minded, *they'll* remember it.
EDWARD:	That's it:
	Yet we are not broken-hearted,
	Neither are we up the spout.
FREDERICA:	Or schoolboy enough.
ROBERT:	Auntie Rachel has just farted,
	Blown her arsehole inside out.
EDWARD:	Or—innocent enough.
MARY:	Who needs men?
FREDERICA:	I think—mostly—other men.
MARY:	Perhaps we should do without 'em altogether.
EDWARD:	I hope you all shall.
MARY:	Be careful.
FREDERICA:	Yes. You're all likely to be taken up on it any moment.
EDWARD:	We have looked upwards at the heavens and seen the signs brooding over us, and taken . . . due note.
FREDERICA:	Good. (*To* MARY) Coming for a swim?
MARY:	Oh. I don't know really. I've got an odd sore on my thigh. It doesn't seem to heal.
FREDERICA:	Nothing does here. Come on.
ROBERT:	I think she's a bit self-conscious about it.
FREDERICA:	In front of her sister and her husband—come on. Even the salt water in this sea must have *some* salty old natural antiseptic in it somewhere.
ROBERT:	Do you mind if I have a drink first?
FREDERICA:	If you don't mind waiting for Flash Leroi, the geni of the island.

ROBERT: Oh yes. (*Calls*) LEROI!

FREDERICA: You'll have to do better than that. He'll just pretend he's not heard.

ROBERT: Leroi!

EDWARD: Leroi!

FREDERICA: Either he'll have heard it or we'll be trampled under a turtle stampede.

EDWARD: (*To* MARY) Would you like me to look at that sore place for you?

MARY: No, thanks. I've bought some stuff at the chemist and old Harry's given me something.

FREDERICA: Harry's got more medicines than Edward ever has.

EDWARD: Mostly local herbs and stuff but they're probably more effective than anything you'll buy. He's full of local folk-lore and benevolent withchcraft.

FREDERICA: Harry must be the only American to stay here longer than a week.

EDWARD: Maybe *they're* right.

FREDERICA: Maybe.

MARY: He must be the oldest—I was going to say European—well, resident.

FREDERICA: I think that palm goes to Lamb. He was clattering his golden typewriter out there just after the war.

ROBERT: *Our* war, you mean?

FREDERICA: Yes. Ours.

MARY: That makes Robin and the Brigadier practically newcomers.

EDWARD: Until the next wave. It's what I think they call "ripe for development".

FREDERICA: Nothing heals, everything goes rotten or mildewed. Slimy. It's like a great green bombed garden . . .

ROBERT: Look at those birds.

FREDERICA: Don't *you* start.

ROBERT: What are they, tern?

FREDERICA: We've named them "the duffers".

MARY: Why?

FREDERICA: Mr. and Mrs. Duffer. Because they're so helpless. Helpless and hopeless. They managed to bang out some eggs, half of which I think they broke themselves. They half built a nest, then it blew down. And when they finished one finally they can hardly remember where they put it.

EDWARD: I find that quite likeable.

FREDERICA: I don't know which of them is worse, him or her. Both hopeless.

EDWARD: Tending your own garden's not a bad resort, even if it *is* the last one *and* bombed at that . . .

FREDERICA: Well, if no one's coming, I think I'll have my dip before Robin and the Brigadier come back to tell me I mustn't spoil the lunch.

MARY: I'd come but Alastair's coming and he'll get cross if my hair's all full of salt and greasy.

FREDERICA: Is he coming to crimp your hair?

MARY: Yes. He's doing it this afternoon.

FREDERICA: Would you ask him to do mine? I've nothing to do.

MARY: Right.

EDWARD: I'll come and watch you.

FREDERICA: Just as you like . . .
(EDWARD *follows her off.*)

MARY: Did I say anything?

ROBERT: She's *your* sister.

MARY: I don't know what any of them are thinking. I never have done. Robin or Evangie neither.

ROBERT: Nor does Edward.

MARY: You *are* enjoying yourself?

ROBERT: The fare was expensive. But otherwise it's cheap.

31

	And the company's good.
MARY:	Who?
ROBERT:	*You*, dozey. . . . The one thing about Frederica. She's adroit. She can even make Edward feel he's created a situation when it's all hers. We're all relatively innocent.
MARY:	Do you think anyone's enjoying it?
ROBERT:	Me.
MARY:	And Robin and the Brigadier?
ROBERT:	They have to. They've chosen to live here.
MARY:	Yes. Odd to think of them actually *living* here.
ROBERT:	Improvising. Getting things done. Plumbing, a new bathroom and shower, or extra guest room . . .
MARY:	Yes, but swimming and sunshine.
ROBERT:	Every day.
MARY:	No taxes.
ROBERT:	Hardly.
MARY:	It seemed as if we were all on holiday again at first. . . . Leroi never came.
ROBERT:	I think one day we'll call and he'll not be there. And someone, Robin and the Brigadier anyhow, will be on their own.
MARY:	I think I know what you mean . . .
ROBERT:	Still, as you say, for the meantime, there's still tennis and water-skiing. The Club, long drinks. Golf course.
MARY:	And Americans. Do you think they'll stay?
ROBERT:	The Americans? Oh, build more hotels I dare say.
MARY:	No, Frederica and Edward?
ROBERT:	Don't know. They're rich enough to cut holidays short. Remember, with her, it's all or nothing, and as you can't get all, not really anywhere . . .

(*Enter* ROBIN *and the* BRIGADIER.)

ROBIN: Hullo. Where's everyone gone to?

ROBERT: Your dad's gone for a walk and to buy a new hat against the sun. And Fred and Ted have gone for a dip. At least, *she* has.

ROBIN: What about the others?

MARY: Well, Alastair should be here soon. And I expect Daddy won't be long.

BRIGADIER: Isn't Lamb coming?

MARY: I expect he'll pick up Alastair in his car.

ROBIN: Only the Brigadier's making one of his soufflés and he's already had too much at the airport *and* the Club while I was shopping.

BRIGADIER: I didn't.

ROBERT: Did the old lady get off all right then?

ROBIN: Usual delays.

BRIGADIER: Only thing left over from the *ancien régime* and that's red tape and it grows like flowers in this climate.

ROBIN: Examined her passport, money, search for fire-arms. Everything. She'd even managed to convince herself she'd had a good time before she got there. And then . . .

BRIGADIER: Better see what Leroi's up to. I can get the salad going, at least, and the wine.

ROBIN: I told *him* to do all that.

BRIGADIER: I know. Drinks all charged? Good.
(*He goes out.*)

ROBIN: And there's always Harry. He'll drop in any old time.

MARY: Can I help?

ROBIN: No. You're here to relax. After all, we *live* here. . . . Do you think they're having a good time?

MARY: Frederica?

ROBIN: Yes.

33

ROBERT:	Enormous. . . . You know what people are like.
ROBIN:	That's the trouble. I don't. I just gave up, years ago. Even my sisters, no, mostly my sisters, except perhaps Mary here. And they've given *me* up too.
MARY:	Well, you do live what's called "out of the way".
ROBIN:	I know. But that's why we came here in the first place. Evangie's working on her book I suppose?
MARY:	Somewhere.
ROBIN:	She never seems to let up. I said to her: come for a "holiday".
MARY:	You know Evangie. Work is everything.
ROBIN:	Not if it's never play as well. Worrying about the reviews——
ROBERT:	Which hardly anyone reads anyway.
ROBIN:	Worrying about the next thing she's going to do.
ROBERT:	And the one after that. And after *that*. No one owes *that* to posterity. What does it do for you?
ROBIN:	I think Christopher may be right about the past after all.
MARY:	What do you mean?
ROBIN:	Looking over his shoulder all the time, living off the things Daddy's done, rather than what he's doing himself now.
ROBERT:	Well, the future owes no one a living. After all, it's done nothing for you . . .
ROBIN:	Still, it's a strange thing, giving yourself up to the reputation of an old man. And an old man so demanding . . . and self-protective. It isn't that the old thing is some *giant*.
MARY:	We may not be the judges of that. He's not half bad . . .
ROBERT:	Even if he's only half good, one shouldn't be on trial by one's daughters. It would make parlour King Lears out of a lot of us.

ROBIN: Perhaps having children of your own puts one in a different position to your own father, and that's why Frederica and I are more critical of him.

MARY: I may be just less critical. . . . But Evangie worships him.

ROBERT: That might be because she feels in blood competition.

ROBIN: As a writer too.

MARY: *His* achievement.

ROBIN: An example.

ROBERT: Of excellence. Or, as you say, *nudging* it.

ROBIN: Christopher feels that obviously. Robert, as someone said, if you've no world of your own, it's rather pleasant to regret the passing of someone else's.

MARY: I think Evangie's a bit keen on him.

ROBIN: Is she really? I'd have thought he wasn't successful enough, too much of a disused hulk. Anyway, I can't see Christopher turning his head forward to an affair with someone like Evangie.

MARY: Or marriage?

ROBIN: Least of all. He's left that behind him. Just so much discarded wreckage and messy debris. Like bits of old cars dumped in the woods.

MARY: I can't think he can feel as bleak as all that, otherwise he couldn't be so cheerful at devoting all his time to Daddy and nannying him like he does.

ROBERT: I don't know. It might be a case of fatigue. Shaky structure. Apologetic for what one is, afraid of what we may become.

MARY: You make him sound such a mediocrity.

ROBERT: I don't think he is. He may want too much, and unlike Evangie, he's given up. People do sometimes choose mediocrity.

35

MARY: But can you really *choose* it?

ROBERT: I don't see why not. It's a way out of feeling isolated. Like a horse's twitch, you apply pain to the nose—to divert it from the knife cutting into it from behind. Or wherever it may be . . .

ROBIN: I think if he's got eyes for anyone, it's Frederica.

ROBERT: Not much joy there, I'd have thought.

ROBIN: No. She and Edward are at least matched.

ROBERT: That would be swapping one twitch for another. She'd eat him before breakfast.

ROBIN: I don't know about that. But it would certainly be hurtful all round. Still, I've watched him with her. He's certainly fascinated by all those straight, masculine gestures of hers and what he thinks is openness.

ROBERT: Instead of a disguise?

ROBIN: Yes.

MARY: Do you imagine Edward's noticed?

ROBIN: Probably. But she knows there's not much pain she can cause there. Besides, I don't think she has much regard for Chris. Though, that might not matter of course.

ROBERT: Could be the opposite.

ROBIN: And, he may be, even he, well, getting a bit tired of coping with the old man . . . I say, we do observe one another and speculate and chatter on about the others.

ROBERT: Perhaps it's being sisters. All four of you. Even to an outsider, there's something fascinating to watch in it. An inner circle of lives. One's almost tempted to try each one in turn.

MARY: Not any more, I hope.

ROBERT: I'm too near the circle.

ROBIN: Yes. And sharing the same parents. But all different.

MARY:	And living different lives, having husbands and lovers or not, or children or not.
ROBERT:	In-laws.
ROBIN:	Don't. At least I know mine's safely on the plane for another twelve months anyway. Sometimes I don't give the Brigadier her letters to him. It often kills the morning. He sits out in his old shed, brooding and smoking and then drinks too much of his own wine for lunch and has to lie down for the rest of the day. What's going on today, anyway?
MARY:	Well, Robert, I expect, will do nothing again. Alastair's coming to do my hair.
ROBIN:	Ah, yes. I hope he doesn't bring anyone. Oh, well, doesn't matter. You all seem to like him.
MARY:	He's thoughtful and attentive. And kind. He amuses Daddy. And the Brigadier likes him. And *he's* keen on Frederica. She's beautiful and she makes *him* laugh.
ROBIN:	And she's got hair he calls "good stuff". Not like my mop.
ROBERT:	Everyone *does* like him. He gives you a feeling he's just about to do or say something brave. Instead of just camp.
MARY:	You're right about Daddy.
ROBERT:	Oh yes, he's always saying to me "When's that nice little queer boy coming round?"
ROBIN:	Yes, he's always asking me the same things about people he's going to meet. "Will I like him?" Then "Is he a bugger or a Jew?"
	(*Enter* CHRISTOPHER *and* EVANGIE.)
CHRISTOPHER:	You're talking about Wyatt. Behind my back.
ROBIN:	Why not? We *have* known him quite a long time.
CHRISTOPHER:	Sure. Longer than I have. Before I'd *heard* of him.

EVANGIE:	He's said that as long as I remember. "Will I like him?" And then "Do you think he'll like *me*?"
CHRISTOPHER:	I've been asleep. Apart from a phone call. Then Evangie's typewriter woke me——
EVANGIE:	Sorry.
CHRISTOPHER:	I should have been up. I made her come out for some sea air. Where's the old boy?
ROBIN:	Up first thing. Gone for his walk. And a new hat. I said I'd throw the old one away.
EVANGIE:	I think he inherited it from George Moore or somebody.
CHRISTOPHER:	Yeats, I think.
EVANGIE:	Oh. Sorry.
CHRISTOPHER:	Don't. It's not very important.
EVANGIE:	It is—to him.
CHRISTOPHER:	Not necessarily.
ROBIN:	Alastair's coming for lunch. Do you want your hair done?
EVANGIE:	Oh, yes.
ROBIN:	What's Wyatt up to after lunch?
CHRISTOPHER:	I've arranged an interview for him. With the island newspaper, whatever it is . . .
MARY:	He'll hate that.
ROBIN:	No he won't. He'll make us and Christopher *think* he does. Or try to.
EVANGIE:	And why not?
ROBERT:	Why not?
CHRISTOPHER:	Indeed.
ROBERT:	You can't make people like Wyatt do things he doesn't really want to do. Even Christopher. It's a mistake one's inclined to make.
	(*Enter* WYATT. *He is about seventy, flushed and hot from his walk.*)
WYATT:	What's that? What are you saying? You can't be talking about me. Gosh, I'm in a soak from all

38

this sun! What a *day* it is! Think of all those people freezing in the Home Counties, hoping the rails and points won't ice up again! Ice and floods to *come*, I dare say. And everybody'll be *so* astonished. As usual. I *have* had a time. Spoke to such a nice lot of people. Charming lot in the shops, and I went to that smashing little market. Got a splendid new hat. Do you like it?

ROBIN: Quite an improvement.

WYATT: Couldn't bear to part with the old one. Poor old thing. They put it in this parcel for me, all done up. Can't remember who gave it me.

EVANGIE: George Moore.

WYATT: No, it wasn't him.

CHRISTOPHER: Yeats.

WYATT: No. Someone . . . I say, you *do* look in the pink, all of you. How nice. You're such a good sight to come back to. I'm quite tired. Been walking since breakfast. Old Leroi can be quite good, you know. I know you don't go on him much but lovely poached eggs he got. Asked him what he thought about the English, and do you know what he said: "I'm glad they've gone, sir, but an English millionaire is still worth more than an American millionaire."

ROBERT: Depends on how many millions.

ROBIN: He means we're better tippers.

WYATT: Went all round the bay. Quite empty. Not an American in sight. Not even old Harry.

ROBIN: He's not exactly a tourist.

WYATT: No. Sweet old thing. Had a good squiz at all the coral. Remarkable. Real Captain Cook, Darwin sort of thing. Saw Nelson's little place. If ever it was, anyway, all jolly nice. What's for lunch?

ROBIN: Salad and soufflé. And some fish. The Brigadier's

	laid it all on today.
WYATT:	Good old Brigadier. Officer material all right. I often think of him in the war and all that. All I ever did was fill in forms for supplies in Delhi most of the time. What have you all been doing?
ROBIN:	Chatting, seeing off mothers . . .
WYATT:	She go off all right?
ROBIN:	Yes, but it seemed like touch and go for a while. When it took off I had a large brandy.
WYATT:	Oh, dear, she's not all that much older than me. I hope you don't have to have large brandies after seeing me off.
ROBIN:	Don't be silly, Papa. You know you're welcome as long as you like.
MARY:	The thing is you're too restless to stay anywhere too long.
EVANGIE:	Besides, you do, at least, seem to enjoy everything—while it lasts, anyway.
ROBERT:	Instead of looking like a professional spare prick at a wedding.
WYATT:	Oh, that *is* good!
MARY:	Robert! Really . . .
WYATT:	Oh, dear, do I seem easily bored? I don't think I am. No, I just like to waddle off in all directions. While I'm still able to. She seemed quite a sprightly old trout. Of course, I suppose we had odd common points of interest, people we both knew. That's one of the things about age, you find less and less people who remember the things you do. Of course, the Brigadier's father was in the Colonial Service, like your grandfather, so there was all that. Then there was the war. She remembered that.
ROBERT:	Yours or ours?
WYATT:	Mine, I suppose, though I don't remember

	much of it. I remember yours, as you call it, all the ration books and being snubbed and kept waiting at the Food Office.
ROBIN:	Don't!
EVANGIE:	Most of the people I meet don't even remember *that*. Or they've forgotten.
MARY:	Or they think you mean Korea or even Vietnam.
WYATT:	Only things I remember well are the list of names of old boys killed or wounded being read out by the Housemaster in chapel. That and being chased by a horde of women, very middle-class sort of women, half way across Southsea because I wasn't in uniform. Jolly thankful I was too. Too feeble to be a conchie and too much of a funk to face all that mud and bullying and limbs blown off. Oh, no. Of course, I was only about fourteen but "tall for my age", as they said then. "Outgrowing my strength". School was bad enough, at least I suppose it wasn't *quite* as bad. Do you know, I was asking the Brigadier the other day why this house was called "Mesopotamia"? Apparently, his father was there in 1917 or whenever it was. Always thought if I'd had to go, or be dragged off, I'd rather have gone there. Expect I'd have been stung by a wasp and died like poor little R. Brooke. Funny end for a poet, I mean *genuinely* funny. I think I'd prefer to be stung to death rather than to wake up in some agonising ward with half of me shot away and the rest in torment. Don't you?
ROBERT:	Right. What school *did* you go to?
WYATT:	Marlborough. That was *my* Western Front. Perhaps it wasn't so bad, though all the ones I've spoken to who were there then who say

they were happy are the most awful types. Overweaning little swots or thumping great Prussian sons of Great Albion. All become florid M.P.s or sarky-tongued bullies at the Bar; clammy old bishops and archbishops or those huge surgeons who tower over you in green and rubber wellies and call their patients "the meat". Of course I was the only one who didn't go to Eton. My father went, so did all my elder brothers.

CHRISTOPHER: Why was that?

WYATT: For one thing I was a skinny, runtish thing, although I was tall and none of my brothers' clothes ever fitted me. Because, of course, being the last, I wore their cast-off jackets and even trousers. Always had a patch on sleeves just below the elbows, so I always felt cold and had chilblains. Anyway, Father decided I needed "toughening up" at a really tough school. *Actually* it was because he'd already sent five sons to Eton and the year I left my prep school, the roof of the house had to be completely re-newed and the old boy said he couldn't afford the fees at Eton, even with reductions. So: that's how I got to Marlborough. Though I believe it's quite a jolly place nowadays, pop music and even girls, girls! What it *could* have been like! Do you know what the cure for chilblains was then? Soaking your feet and hands in your own pee. *Most* unpleasant—you ponged all over the class-room and weren't even warm when you dunked yourself.

ROBIN: Well, *I'd* better rescue the Brigadier from Leroi. I hope Frederica isn't too late for lunch. The old chap gets awfully upset if his cooking is spoiled.

MARY:	Start without them.
ROBIN:	No. He likes everyone to sit down.
WYATT:	Quite right. We'll wait for her. I say, the old boy's jolly clever with his cooking, isn't he? Must be nice for you, old thing. I could never cook an *egg*, not even at Oxford, where everybody seemed to.
ROBIN:	Well, it's better than relying on *my* cooking and anything's better than Leroi. You'll get lunch about tea time.
CHRISTOPHER:	Shall I go and look for Frederica?
ROBIN:	No, she'll come in her own time. Edward's with her, anyway. He'll hurry her somehow.
CHRISTOPHER:	Pretty exhausting—hurrying people up. Like picking up a child's clothes for him.
MARY:	*You* should know . . .
EVANGIE:	I think when you love someone you should do so, knowing that one day you will hate them.
WYATT:	I say, *what* an interesting remark!
EVANGIE:	I've seen it happen too often——
MARY:	To others?
EVANGIE:	Most of us.
WYATT:	Do you know, I haven't thought of it? I suppose I must be a thundering old nuisance. Am I, Christopher?
CHRISTOPHER:	You're scrupulous about the things that matter.
WYATT:	No, Evangie's right as usual.
EVANGIE:	I wish I *were* "right as usual".
CHRISTOPHER:	Do you? I don't. But I don't expect it. Certainly not of myself.
WYATT:	No. I *am* disorganized. I forget things, leave things about, crash in everywhere, like some maddening old toddler. I *must* watch it. Otherwise, you'll *all* need large brandies when you see the back of me. . . . Your mother was a bit

like that and I never realized it till she was dead. I must have enjoyed a few brandies since that funeral. Awful thing to say, but I think that was almost the most enjoyable day of my life. When those ropes slid down into that grave, I had to lower my head right down so that no one could see my face . . . I must be very unfeeling indeed, I mean not to feel anything but, no not relief, merriment, that's the word for it, merriment at my own wife's funeral! Even good old Cranmer's words didn't affect me. Well, of course, none of you really remember her. Except Robin, I suppose?

ROBIN: Not much. Try and hurry them up.
            (*She goes out.*)

WYATT: Is that nice little queer boy coming?

MARY: Yes. He's crimping the entire family.

WYATT: Oh, good. I do like him. I didn't know whatsit, crimping, was such an interesting business. Like being in the mess or common room. Wish he'd do *mine*. He's got a splendid head of hair.

MARY: It's a wig.

WYATT: Good heavens—a wig! Is it really?

MARY: Yes, *really*, Daddy.

WYATT: Perhaps he'd get *me* one. How do you *know* it is?

MARY: Some of us do notice these things.

WYATT: Did *you* know?

EVANGIE: Yes.

WYATT: Robert?

ROBERT: Yes, but he told me too. First time we met he said "You know I'm just an uptight little bald Scots queen under this red rug. They all send me up and call me either the Virgin Queen or Mary, Queen of Scots! It used to upset me but now I'm not bothered."

44

WYATT: Did he say that? Poor little devil! I suppose he must really be bothered, in fact.

EVANGIE: It's not only hairdressing that's cut-throat in his line.

WYATT: Yes, I see what you mean. Gosh, I'm so glad I didn't mention it to him. It would have seemed most unkind. I wish I noticed things like *you* all do.

MARY: I think you do, really, Daddy. You don't miss the tricks.

WYATT: Devious, you mean? Yes. I see you do. That's not a nice trait either. Pretending not to notice, when all the time you do.

EVANGIE: We forgive you.

MARY: Like your calling Robin "old thing".

WYATT: But I call everyone "old thing". Why, oh, even Leroi.

MARY: Exactly, it makes her feel old.

WYATT: It's just that she *is* the oldest of you all.

MARY: And inferior and played out.

WYATT: I honestly didn't mean to . . .

MARY: Whether you did or didn't, it still sounds disparaging and unkind. To her, anyway.

WYATT: Oh dear, I am sorry. You make me feel quite awful.

MARY: Like you never call Frederica "old thing" or me even. Or call her Fred, Fred and Ted, like some do, because you know she hates it. She gets "lovely long legs and hair like your mother . . ."

WYATT: Do I do that? Oh, dear. Poor old Robin. There I go again! It's just that I think of you all differently, different parts of my life. Robin, well, the eldest, first born then, you the young, pretty one with your own babies, and Evangie, the intellectual one.

45

EVANGIE: Thanks. I know what a pejorative "intellectual" is to you.

WYATT: Not at all. I'm just frightened of people who are cleverer than me. They are even worse than the physical bullies at school. You could always *despise* them, even when they were making you cry.

EVANGIE: Men don't want "intellectual" daughters any more than they do wives.

WYATT: Oh, my dear, I seem to have hurt you all. I never meant to . . .

EVANGIE: Not Frederica. She was the only one who couldn't care.

WYATT: It's just that a lot of things I don't understand, and I suppose I've stepped over them or discarded them like my boots on the floor. I never even knew what "growing out of your strength" meant when it was said to me as a boy. Though I said it to Evangie, I know. Oh, dear. . . . This hat's not as good as the old one. I feel quite hot. I'd better go into the shade, I think . . .

MARY: Alastair's probably coming with Lamb.

WYATT: Lamb? What's that?

MARY: The writer.

EVANGIE: Is he? Gosh, how good.

WYATT: Not a *writer*? Oh, Lord, I hate meeting writers.

EVANGIE: But why?

WYATT: They *know* about you usually. They can trip you up if they've a mind to. If they're better than me, I get all yellowy and envious, and if they're worse it just depresses me. For them. And then again, if they're bad, they perform themselves so *well* and amuse everyone. And if they're really good, they don't bother to perform at all, quite rightly, all lordly. Oh dear, Lamb is it? But he's

	frightfully successful, isn't he, invented tax havens and things and writes best sellers?
CHRISTOPHER:	I shouldn't worry about all that. Anyway, he's quite shy.
WYATT:	Is he a bugger?
CHRISTOPHER:	Almost certainly.
EVANGIE:	But not necessarily literally.
MARY:	And not Jewish.
WYATT:	Is that why he's coming with little Alastair?
EVANGIE:	Possibly. Alastair would tell you if you ask him.
WYATT:	Oh no. How awful. I wonder if he takes his wig off in bed. Lamb . . . Lamb. I remember him. We got frightfully drunk together in some club somewhere years ago. Savile or somewhere like that. But he's frightfully impressive. Rather good too, they tell me. I remember he asked me why I pretended to be an ageing schoolboy all the time and I was so embarrassed I didn't go out for a month afterwards. Then he said to me "How queer are you?" And I was so nonplussed because we didn't talk about that much at that time. So, like an awful coward, because I was pretty sure he *was*, I said a bit too airily, "Oh, about forty-five per cent." And he said "Are you? How interesting, I'm ninety-five. You see, I don't trust women." And I said something foolish and gauche. Like "Oh, but all your best friends must have been women."
ROBERT:	What did *he* say?
WYATT:	"Oh *exactly*", or something of the sort. I was so confused by him. Do you think he'll remember?
EVANGIE:	Might do.
WYATT:	Oh, dear. He must have thought me the most unbearable little prig. I do hope he doesn't. I mean he's really *famous*, isn't he?

CHRISTOPHER: Not in the way *you* are, and he'll know it.

WYATT: You know, I thought of him then as being lots older than me, but, if anything, I suppose he's even a bit younger. He wasn't at Marlborough, I do remember. Eton or Winchester, much grander altogether.

CHRISTOPHER: Don't worry. He'll be more worried than you are. Anyway, you've got this interview this afternoon.

WYATT: What interview?

CHRISTOPHER: With the island newspaper.

WYATT: Oh no, I say, can't we cancel it?

CHRISTOPHER: He sounds quite a nice young man.

WYATT: Can't put him off? Oh, he'll expect me to be clever and say witty things instead of just being an old duffer who happens to be a writer.

EVANGIE: I think you'll manage.

MARY: Just say all the things you usually say. They won't have heard them out here.

WYATT: What a good wheeze! After all, they all ask the same questions, like have you moved further to the Right; should writers be seen on television; are they any longer relevant to the global village, wherever that is; or just plain do you use a pen or a typewriter? Is he a native? An islander?

CHRISTOPHER: Well, he—she's not English.

WYATT: Then she should be all right I'd think.

CHRISTOPHER: As Mary says, it doesn't matter, anyway.

ROBERT: If it doesn't matter, why does he need to do it?

WYATT: Look a bit childish I suppose. And you know how sensitive they can be in these little places. Especially ex-colonies or whatever they're called.

EVANGIE: Independent states.

WYATT: That's right.

(*Enter* ALASTAIR *with* JED. *Both in their early twenties, but* JED *with shoulder-length black hair. Behind them is* LAMB, *expensively dressed and with a club tie.*)

ALASTAIR: Don't talk to me about independent states. This place is just Tel Aviv, U.S.A. in Atlantic. Have you seen that lot come in this morning on that boat? My dear, they've been in all morning in their mickey mouse glasses and Florida Blue dilly-dilly hairdo's. As if I'd touch the one of them. Complaining and carrying on, they didn't like Fiji, they liked Australia better. *Australia!* All those beaches, none of which they'd dare go near, but India was worse, and, as for *Europe*, that was worse, even the culture they didn't see much of. Or *think* much of, anyway. Talk about your Young Geriatrics Tours, Inc. "Can you tell me the way to the Gift Shop, young man? Oh, because we've lost our tour guide." I wish we'd lose *them!*

WYATT: Oh, Alastair! How nice it is to see you! You *are* a jolly old thing. *Do* tell us about the Americans.

ALASTAIR: Don't ask—oh, well I'm bound to bore you about it, anyway. They just make me *mad. You* know. Oh, I don't think you know Mr. Lamb, any of you?

WYATT: My dear Lamb, how nice, what a pleasure to see you here. Do you remember? I was just saying— we met once and got awfully drunk and sorry for ourselves at the Savile—or was it the Travellers?

LAMB: Somewhere like that.

WYATT: This is my daughter, Evangie and my youngest, Mary. That's her old man, Robert. Seems a bit

49

	surly when you first talk to him but he's North Country, East Riding I think, *and* a schoolteacher so it's not all his fault and he's a cracking good sort underneath it all, aren't you, old thing?
ROBERT:	A little cracker.
WYATT:	Then there's Frederica, my other daughter and her husband, Eddie. But they're down at the beach. She's rather beautiful, but I'm not supposed to say it and *you* certainly mustn't. She's a frightful flirt, even with me and I know she doesn't care for me over much. Evangie, she's awfully brainy and *writes*. She'll probably trap you in a corner, so I should watch it. Mary's the youngest and prettiest and quite the least trouble of any of them, enjoys everything, doesn't carp, well not much, does as she's told and smiles and has lots of lovely little kiddies, which the others don't and who can blame them if they're as selfish as me? I never bothered with *my* children. Some people would say I was selfish and maybe it's so but I've always been fascinated by myself long after everyone else was bored to death with me.
ALASTAIR:	Stop it! How can you *do* it in this weather?
WYATT:	Who else is there? Oh, old Harry. He's not here yet but we think he'll turn up sometime. He's an American but not like the others at all.
LAMB:	I know.
WYATT:	Well, of course, you must know him better than any of us.
ALASTAIR:	This is Jed. He's a student. He's just on his way.
WYATT:	How do you do, Jed. Where are you on your way to?
JED:	Wherever . . .

WYATT: Yes. I know what you mean. When Alastair says
                you are a student, are you an eternal student
                like, say, Trefimov?

ALASTAIR: He's an eternal student, you can take it from
                me. Shall we get ourselves a drink inside? I'll
                have a word with Robin to let her know we're
                here. Is she with Leroi and the Brigadier? Oh,
                she'll be wanting help then.
                (*The three of them,* ALASTAIR, JED *and* LAMB, *go in.*)

MARY: (*after them*) I expect lunch is ready.

WYATT: Was I all right?

CHRISTOPHER: Fine. He was nervous. I think I'll go and see if
                I can find Frederica and Edward.

MARY: I shouldn't worry. They'll come if they want.

CHRISTOPHER: I'll just have a look. All right, Wyatt?

WYATT: Fine, dear boy, fine. Oh, I say, I forgot to
                introduce you.

CHRISTOPHER: It doesn't matter.
                (*He goes off.*)

WYATT: Do you think I hurt his feelings?

EVANGIE: No.

WYATT: I do hope not. He's such a dear boy.

MARY: Let's go in. I'm hungry.

ROBERT: Me too.

EVANGIE: Right.
                (*They rise.*)

WYATT: I feel a bit tired. Anyway, I think I'll wait for
                Christopher and Frederica.

EVANGIE: Just as you like.

WYATT: Won't be a jiffy . . .
                (*They go off. He closes his eyes for a few moments.
                Then opens them as* HARRY, *an enormous figure in
                late middle age, comes in.*)
                Harry, my dear boy. We were talking of you.

HARRY: Yes? Americans, I suppose?

51

(*He lowers his great frame into a chair.*)
Ah! That's better.

WYATT: Not like *you*, Harry. Not like you. You're *special*.

HARRY: That's what we're here for, Wyatt. That's what we're here for.

WYATT: Are you all right? You look awfully tired.

HARRY: I'm O.K. You know. You get, just tired, and in this climate . . .

WYATT: Yes. I know what you mean, old thing. I wonder where Frederica's got to . . . I miss the cold and the damp and the colours that change all the winter and then . . . I miss it . . . I wish I didn't . . .

HARRY: Well, guess I'd better make myself known to Robin and the Brigadier and warn 'em I'm here. (*He rises*) You coming?

WYATT: Later, dear boy. I think I'll wait a little longer.

HARRY: O.K. You'll miss the Brigadier's *plat de maison*. (*He goes into the house.*)
(WYATT *closes his eyes against the sun.*)

END OF ACT ONE

ACT TWO

After lunch. The same scene. Resting in the shade are WYATT, ROBERT, CHRISTOPHER, LAMB *and* EVANGIE. *Only* FREDERICA *is standing, looking across the bay.*

WYATT: (*presently*) I *thought* this new hat was a mistake.

FREDERICA: Sit in the shade, you old silly.

WYATT: Oh, *aren't I*? (*He moves his chair*) Gosh, it's a scorcher!

FREDERICA: There's a great breeze if you stand up here.

WYATT: Couldn't stand anywhere after all that lunch the Brigadier got for us. I say, he *is* hot stuff in that department, isn't he? But he *was* quite a soldier.

FREDERICA: I suppose it usually is.

WYATT: What?

FREDERICA: Quite a scorcher. Here.

WYATT: Oh.

LAMB: There's a cool season. It rains and there's mist and the mildew sprouts for a few weeks. But it never lasts long.

WYATT: (*re-settled*) Oh yes, that's more like it.

ROBERT: It'll be cold at home.

WYATT: Perishing. Nice though.

FREDERICA: What are you thinking about?

WYATT: Me?

FREDERICA: Anyone. Don't go to sleep. Robert, keep awake.

ROBERT: Sorry. I was trying *not* to think about the new term starting next week. Breath on the grey playground, frozen lavatories and Irish stew and

53

	sweating middens of cabbage.
WYATT:	My dear boy! Don't! How awful for you.
FREDERICA:	They're only children.
ROBERT:	We're all children once.
FREDERICA:	What a pious remark. We may be, but some are more so than others. And leave it behind more quickly.
ROBERT:	I'm sorry I sounded pious.
FREDERICA:	Now you're piqued.
WYATT:	I didn't think so at all.
LAMB:	No. It's like saying: what's 1950 got to do with 1980?
FREDERICA:	Well, *what*?
LAMB:	We'll be the same people.
FREDERICA:	Will we? What were *you* thinking?
LAMB:	What I usually think of after lunch here. Walking down Bond Street in mid-afternoon with a nice evening to look forward to at Covent Garden or somewhere and time for tea at the Ritz and money to buy myself a present or, even better, someone else as well.
FREDERICA:	Daddy?
WYATT:	Blackfriars Station and George Moore.
FREDERICA:	You're making it up.
WYATT:	No, I'm not. I was thinking of the beastly cold like Robert. Of waiting for trains and then looking up at the front of Blackfriars Station and seeing it inscribed in the stone: Broadstairs; Dresden; Cheltenham; and *St. Petersburg*. So I asked the booking clerk for a cheap return to St. Petersburg.
ROBERT:	What did he say?
WYATT:	"I'm afraid you'll have to go to Victoria."
LAMB:	When was this?
WYATT:	Nineteen sixty-one. What was the other thing?

ROBERT:	George Moore.
WYATT:	Nothing. I did meet him a couple of times when I was a young man. Ebury Street, I think, he lived. Anyway, he always looked dreadfully ill at ease in company, especially mixed company, keeping his hands in his pockets all the time. And one day someone asked him why and he said: "Well you see, whenever I stand up I'm afraid my underpants will fall down and it's a very uncomfortable feeling in company. Especially mixed company." And so, whoever it was, said: "But George, do you not have those little tabs inside to put your braces through?" And Moore replied: "Oh—*those*. Do you know I've always been wondering what those were for!"
FREDERICA:	I know why you like that story.
ROBERT:	Why? I'd not heard it.
FREDERICA:	Because he likes writers being made out to be divine simpletons or holy innocents, and himself most of all.
WYATT:	Unholy. I think we're a dismal bunch, on the whole, to meet, anyway. Don't you think so?
LAMB:	The *performers* are the worst.
WYATT:	That's true enough! Indeed. When I think . . . I was dreading meeting *you*. What a relief it's turned out. He's a modest old thing, don't you think?
LAMB:	I'm not proud of living out in the sunshine if you mean that?
WYATT:	Certainly not. Where people choose to live is their own business.
ROBERT:	Listen . . .
FREDERICA:	Not those bloody birds?
ROBERT:	The surf.

FREDERICA:	What about it?
ROBERT:	I can't get used to the sound of it.
FREDERICA:	I can. That's the trouble.
WYATT:	Not like Cornwall.
ROBERT:	Or Pembroke.
FREDERICA:	Or Northumberland. Or Brighton. Do *shut up*, both of you! You're being like those people who are never bored again and we know what a deadly lot those are.
LAMB:	It makes quite a fair old row——
FREDERICA:	In the wet season.
ROBERT:	Robin's never bored.
FREDERICA:	No. She never was.
ROBERT:	Neither's the Brigadier.
WYATT:	No. Not him.
ROBERT:	Cooking.
FREDERICA:	Washing up.
ROBERT:	Digging, watching his vines and waterfalls and rock gardens.
FREDERICA:	Smoking his pipe. I wish men wouldn't smoke pipes.
WYATT:	Oh, don't you like it? You used to say you liked the smell of mine.
FREDERICA:	I did. I do. It's just *some* men. The way they *do* it. Putting you in your place . . .
ROBERT:	Watching, observing, feeding the lizards——
WYATT:	Oh, birds. Birds of boredom. What does that make me think of?
FREDERICA:	Trafalgar Square. . . . How strange you all seem sometimes.
LAMB:	We are. And not. And you?
FREDERICA:	I don't feel that. No. Not at all.
WYATT:	Tedious flight of tern, How I wonder what you'd earn.
ROBERT:	Did you make that up?

FREDERICA:	What else?
WYATT:	If you fumbled in the sky for words
	Would you still just bore like birds? . . .
ROBERT:	Good.
WYATT:	No. . . . Chatter. Frederica is right as usual. Birds chatter and *that* is their mortal flaw. Chatter sins against language and when we sin against the word, we sin against God. Gosh, I *am* pompous.
FREDERICA:	I wasn't going to say it.
WYATT:	Must be the Brigadier's cuddly, loving little grape. Where's your old man got to?
FREDERICA:	He's out there on the beach talking to Jed.
LAMB:	Oh, *does* he talk?
ROBERT:	I think *there is* someone who could sin against language if he could bring himself to it.
WYATT:	Do you, really? Seemed a quiet little chap to me. I tried talking to him but he never said a word.
FREDERICA:	Why should he? He despises us.
WYATT:	Oh, do you think he does? Yes. Of course. You're right. Oh, dear. . . . Perhaps I said the wrong thing . . . I only asked him about himself.
FREDERICA:	He doesn't want your interest. Or anyone's.
WYATT:	I thought dear little Alastair was his chum.
FREDERICA:	He despises him too.
WYATT:	What a shame. Perhaps I should try again?
FREDERICA:	Don't. Anyway, you know you've no intention. You dislike him as much as the rest of us. No. More. He frightens you more.
WYATT:	I wonder if I should have a sleep and then a walk. Or a walk and *then* a sleep. What do you think?
FREDERICA:	Either. On the other hand: both.
ROBERT:	The first. Except chatter a bit.
WYATT:	Oh. Shall I? I'll annoy old Fred there.
FREDERICA:	Would that stop you? I wonder if you can get lung cancer from smoking pot?

ROBERT:	Ask Jed.
FREDERICA:	I will. There's something about that boy . . .
ROBERT:	What?
FREDERICA:	I don't know. But he shouldn't *be* here.
LAMB:	Well, he is. And plenty more.
FREDERICA:	I shan't be sorry to leave this place.
WYATT:	Well, don't let old Robin and the Brigadier know.
FREDERICA:	Oh, I know. They've taken such pains to give us a good time.
ROBERT:	And they live here.
FREDERICA:	I'm sorry. I know. And so do you. (*To* LAMB.)
LAMB:	That's all right, my dear. I see everyone think it. The ones who come to visit, I mean. Friends. They sit in the sun, and are waited on and bathe and chat, barefoot on the white evening sand, watching the sea and—thinking . . .
ROBERT:	That they're glad not to be you.
LAMB:	Not to be rich enough to be an exile, browned and attended on by sun and by the regular wind and service. But back to cold, uncertain tides and striving pavements. And the marriage of anxieties . . . domestic . . . oh . . . extremes . . .
FREDERICA:	Where were you born?
LAMB:	Me? Kuala Lumpur. Natch.
FREDERICA:	Yes. But it doesn't—warm you—as it should do. No. It leaves you open to all the chills when you come back . . . over the other side.
LAMB:	You?
FREDERICA:	Kandy. Ceylon . . . Robin too.
LAMB:	You?
EVANGIE:	Singapore.
ROBERT:	As they used to say, "their father had a bike".
WYATT:	What's that?
EVANGIE:	Grandpa was in "the Service".
WYATT:	Papa? Oh, I'll say he was.

ROBERT: Where were *you* born?

WYATT: Srinigar. Kashmir. Shalimar. Bit like the Thames near Henley. Lots of lush and vegetables and Weybridge-type curry and pink blancmange in little elephant moulds. Oh, the old boy wanted *me* to go in it, of course. All I did was sire four daughters at his various postings. Trying to be *A* Writer. But you *can* write and give Some Service as well. Give some service. Well, I never did. Just his non-paying guest. With a wife and four thumping daughters. Well—*he* gave service. Old thing . . .

LAMB: And your husband?

FREDERICA: Rangoon.

WYATT: What about you, old thing?

ROBERT: Hastings Royal Infirmary.

WYATT: Hastings Royal Infirmary! What about the Brigadier? Where do you suppose *he* was born?

FREDERICA: Mesopotamia.

WYATT: Mesopotamia. Of *course*.

ROBERT: That's why the house is named.

WYATT: To: Mesopotamia. You can see him . . . setting out. Or someone . . .

FREDERICA: I wish Edward would stop talking to that boy. Man . . .

WYATT: Who? Little Alastair?

FREDERICA: No. Not little Alastair. Jed.

ROBERT: Perhaps it's his scientific curiosity: "the young mind".

FREDERICA: No. The young, whatever they are, bore him even more than I do.

WYATT: My darling Fred, he adores you.

FREDERICA: Maybe. But he's not a pathologist for nothing.

ROBERT: Examining blood.

FREDERICA: All day.

59

EVANGIE:	Frederica's right.
WYATT:	Of course. She always is.
EVANGIE:	About being born. Away from home.
FREDERICA:	Home?
EVANGIE:	Whatever . . .
WYATT:	Out of all . . . hearts . . .
EVANGIE:	Do you remember Grandfather's study?
WYATT:	What? The old boy's?
FREDERICA:	I'll say.
WYATT:	All my life . . .
EVANGIE:	The joss sticks and Burmese guns. Saddle oil...
FREDERICA:	Even the books smelt of curry powder. The Casino Palace, Port Said.
EVANGIE:	Back numbers of the *Times of Natal*. A Zulu grammar.
FREDERICA:	Manuals in Urdu.
EVANGIE:	Rawhide shields and dried python skins and brass iguanas. And the photographs.
FREDERICA:	Brown. Brown to yellow.
WYATT:	The Casino Palace!
EVANGIE:	The Groups.
WYATT:	What did the old boy say? I know—"The Royal Navy always travels first class".
EVANGIE:	Probyn's Horse, the Peshewar Vale Hunt, tennis parties.
WYATT:	Signed photograph of Lord Minto.
EVANGIE:	Tent pegging. "Robin: aged one year". A cricket match on the parade ground; amateur theatricals.
FREDERICA:	Mummy as Lydia Languish in *The Rivals*.
WYATT:	Daddy on the prompt book.
EVANGIE:	Field batteries, elephant batteries! I never understood them going into torches. . . . The Newcastle Mounted Rifles.
FREDERICA:	Inspected by Grandfather. Men *do* inspect.
ROBERT:	England Inspects . . .

EVANGIE:	Frederica on Grandmother's pony.
FREDERICA:	In a white party frock.
EVANGIE:	A timetable of the South India Railway, the oars of Jesus College; *In China with the British*—two vols. "Setting sail aboard the *Rawalpindi*".
WYATT:	Old *Pindi*—torpedoed first month of the war.
EVANGIE:	Taking arsenic instead of baking powder. Talk in the mess. The club.
FREDERICA:	In the club. Mummy four times. Lizards on the ceiling above the mosquito net, sweat, the mail. Knick-knacks. Junk and boa constrictors . . .
WYATT:	I'm surprised you remember so much. *I* don't. You were all such *children* . . .
FREDERICA:	Ah—home to England.
WYATT:	*I* don't. At least I don't think so. Do I? Yes. I suppose so. I took it for granted then. Busy being a "writer". God, Lamb, why do we do it?
LAMB:	For the money. And being treated well, or better than you *should* be by any rights . . .
FREDERICA:	The sky is *so* clear . . . the trees seem even darker than they are. . . . What was it like before?
LAMB:	Before? Oh, not so very different I suppose. The Governor General's house is still there though he's called something else now; Royalty of some sort came out. New flag went up. The police band played the dreadful National Anthem, all deliciously out of tune; you couldn't believe it, the comedy and pain of it. I think someone actually recorded it as a collector's item. Some relief, I suppose. A bit of apprehension but not over much. The climate was the same, the people were the same, we were the same. Except. . . . You see. . . . There was despair in a lot of hearts. Even in those who . . . who . . . oh, who . . .
WYATT:	Yes. I can see all that. Can't you? The lady-in-

	waiting; the umbrellas; the marquee.
LAMB:	It was comic then. And it's comic *now*. If anyone could ever think of it or remember it. But it was full of pain. *And* some quite good people. Thing about pain. It changes as *you* change. But it doesn't go, does it? *Does* it? Or am I mad as I often think I am when I'm alone, or begging Robin and the Brigadier's pardon? . . .
WYATT:	You're not mad, old thing . . .
LAMB:	Wish you weren't all going.
WYATT:	Still a bit of time.
LAMB:	There's me and Robin. The Brigadier. Alastair chatting up the tourists in his crimping parlour. Going on his crying jags, threatening us all with his too many sleeping pills, falling in love with young Americans he despises and who despise him. Looking to an Old Etonian queen like me, who's respectable only because he's rich and famous. Turning to Jed, who hates him slightly less than the rest of us . . .
WYATT:	Oh dear . . .
LAMB:	Mortified by the sunlight on his wig join.
FREDERICA:	That could have been a song once. When you think of it. "Sunlight On My Wig Join".
LAMB:	I'm sorry.
FREDERICA:	No.
LAMB:	It's just that we shall miss you. But I shouldn't have really said so.
FREDERICA:	Why not? You *thought* it.
LAMB:	Do *you* say everything you think?
FREDERICA:	No. People think I do. Sometimes *I* think I do.
LAMB:	Robin will miss you.
ROBERT:	Sisters are strange things.
FREDERICA:	We all travesty ourselves. It seems unavoidable. Totally . . .

WYATT: (*reading paper*) Good God!
LAMB: What?
WYATT: Do you know what we're missing on B.B.C.! At this almost very moment? Robert, *you* read it. You've got good, young eyes.
ROBERT: (*reads*) "Europe Since 1945. The fifth of twelve programmes on economic and social change in Western and Eastern Europe since the end of the Second World War. Next: New Structures in Society . . ."
LAMB: Oh, no . . .
ROBERT: "To what extent have such factors as economic growth increased educational opportunity, and welfare of post-European societies both east and west, towards a single type of industrial society? . . ."
FREDERICA: Help!
ROBERT: "By the Professor of Social and Industrial Studies at the Sorbonne. *Worker Participation Control:* A discussion of different forms of worker power in industrial management, from participation French style, through West German co-operation to Yugoslavia's worker-control. Thursday: Managing the economy Number Seven. Prospects for an Incomes Policy. How to contain rising prices is something that has baffled one government after another . . ."
WYATT: Baffled!
FREDERICA: Stop!
LAMB: Oh, yes. Please.
ROBERT: "Does the present exercise in regulating prices and incomes offer any real chance of a breakthrough?"
FREDERICA: Can't wait! Let's go home *now*.
ROBERT: "*People in Towns.*" Urban Sociology. A course.

The existence of social problems in our towns has produced its equal and opposite reaction—the social work movement.

FREDERICA: Even the birds look good after that.

ROBERT: "The Lecturer for Social Work Training . . ."

WYATT: Social Work Training?

ROBERT: "Talks about——"

WYATT: What does the Old Thing talk about?

ROBERT: "About social workers and about the work of the Seebohm Committee, of which he was a member . . ."

FREDERICA: Poor soul.

ROBERT: "Further publications relating to this series include: *Second Year Russian*. Eight shillings. *Starting German*. Books One and Two, price four shillings each. *Europe Since 1945*. *Study Notes I*, five shillings. *Study Notes II*, seven shillings. *People in Towns* will cost you eighteen shillings. *Manet* (colour slides) two pounds; *Renaissance Exploration*, eleven shillings; *Helping Your Neighbour*, three shillings and *Problems of Learning, Study Notes*, three shillings."

WYATT: My goodness! What you're missing, old thing!

ROBERT: Mustn't be patronizing now.

FREDERICA: Why not? I'm always being patronizing.

ROBERT: That's because you're more clever and assured than most people.

FREDERICA: Oh no, I'm not. Evangie's the clever one.

EVANGIE: I'm not. Still a lot of people do. . . . No, I won't say it.

LAMB: Why not?

EVANGIE: Because it sounds priggish and what people think I am.

LAMB: Which is?

EVANGIE: A rather voracious intellectual.

WYATT: Oh, come!

EVANGIE: It's true. Isn't it?

FREDERICA: Yes.

EVANGIE: True—or what people think?

FREDERICA: Both I should think. Don't ask me. They're all cleverer than I am . . .

WYATT: I rather like "*Helping Your Neighbour*" *Study Notes* . . .

EVANGIE: No. I'm sure you're right.

FREDERICA: You said it.

EVANGIE: And you agreed.

FREDERICA: Shouldn't I?

EVANGIE: Yes. I think you should. It's hard on me but probably harder for you.

FREDERICA: It's not hard at all.

EVANGIE: Then it should be. Even if it is your sister. . . . I'm off to the beach I think. Daddy?

WYATT: Think I'll stay in the shade a bit, old thing. I'm so *feeble*. We'll have a walk before dinner, right?

EVANGIE: Right.
(*She goes. Pause.*)

FREDERICA: You all think I'm a shit, don't you?

LAMB: *I* don't think so. Not me, anyway. But then I *am*. You're a clown. With all the privileges and penalties. You say what is obvious but not necessarily true, or the whole truth, at least. But that's something else and in the meantime there's the performing dog act of partiality.

FREDERICA: Thanks.

LAMB: Don't thank me. Everyone is grateful to you.

FREDERICA: Meaning?

LAMB: Please don't pick a fight with me, my dear. I like and admire you though, of course, don't know you or ever will. I may not, and I don't wish to, be able to hurt you. But this I do know: that

	nothing you could say or do would ever hurt me. Which is *my* misfortune.
FREDERICA:	That was a bit glib, even for you, wasn't it?
LAMB:	Not really. I tried a little more with you but it didn't come off. Quite clearly . . . I was thinking the other day about moon landings . . .
WYATT:	God, the sun does BURN, doesn't it?
FREDERICA:	The birds *sing*.
ROBERT:	The surf—what? Pounds I suppose.
WYATT:	Why are we all so cruel to one another?
FREDERICA:	*You're* not.
WYATT:	Yes. I am.
FREDERICA:	Yes. You are.
ROBERT:	Frankly.
FREDERICA:	Frankly. But no one thinks you're a shit. They think you're loveable.
LAMB:	Don't be intemperate. You lose your style.
FREDERICA:	I don't know what intemperate means, or what you mean by it and I'm too proud to find out, do you mind? And, as for style, I haven't.
LAMB:	I don't know you any more than I know your father but he has some concern for himself, as we all have. You mustn't grudge that.
FREDERICA:	Why not?
LAMB:	Because I feel it.
FREDERICA:	There! That's all.
LAMB:	Of course, you're right.
WYATT:	She always is.
LAMB:	No more than that.
WYATT:	Always was. Evangie *seemed* the clever one. But she's not, poor old thing. Oh dear, I must stop saying that.
ROBERT:	What?
WYATT:	Old thing.
FREDERICA:	Quite. You should.

66

WYATT:	I know.
FREDERICA:	It isn't half as cute as everyone thinks or thinks they think.
WYATT:	Yes. Pretty nauseating really. Well: I am.
FREDERICA:	Don't sound pleased about it.
WYATT:	I'm not. Actually. I don't quite know how to make it ring true. Or. Indeed . . . anything. I think moon landings must be pretty morose, don't you, I mean as we're being morose and we are, at least I am . . . (*To* CHRISTOPHER) You're very quiet, old thing.
CHRISTOPHER:	Am I?
FREDERICA:	Yes. Exhausted.
CHRISTOPHER:	No. Tired. It's a tiring island.
FREDERICA:	It is. So are we.
WYATT:	Should we get him a doctor?
FREDERICA:	Is that a real question?
CHRISTOPHER:	I'm all right. I was just wondering if I should go for a swim or walk or something with Evangie.
WYATT:	Too hot . . . Phew!
FREDERICA:	She's all right.
CHRISTOPHER:	Is she though?
FREDERICA:	She's thinking about writing a piece about this place. Or some book. Or some insight she's fishing around for.
CHRISTOPHER:	If it's well enough done and for the right reasons.
LAMB:	I never know what the right reasons are.
FREDERICA:	Oh, for *its* sake. And your's. Or neither— Who knows?
LAMB:	Clearly, *you* don't.
ROBERT:	Who would you send to the moon?
FREDERICA:	Oh, the usual. Me, I expect.
WYATT:	Yes, who *would* we?
FREDERICA:	I wonder why people have children. Do they *want* you? What do you think, Robert?

(*At this stage* ROBIN, *the* BRIGADIER, ALASTAIR, JED *and* HARRY *come out on to the porch and join the company*.)

(*To* ROBERT) That man's dying.

ROBERT: Who?

FREDERICA: Harry. The hulking American.

WYATT: There you are, old things. I say, we did have a good lunch. Brigadier, you're a genius. We were just talking about moon landings and who we'd send up there.

ROBIN: Customs officers.

WYATT: Naturally.

LAMB: Women journalists.

WYATT: Good.

ALASTAIR: American tourists.

FREDERICA: But not Harry.

ALASTAIR: Harry's not exactly a tourist. He dropped in with Nelson. Anyone who goes on cruises. Do you know who we've got in today? The American Folk Dance Society. Eight hundred of them?

BRIGADIER: All local officials.

ROBIN: The High Commissioner.

ALASTAIR: The High Commissioner's wife.

FREDERICA: People who give poetry readings.

WYATT: Oh, I say, yes.

(*They all settle into their chairs and relax in the shade*.)

I was just thinking about what the girls were saying.

BRIGADIER: What were they saying?

WYATT: Don't think you were here, old thing. About the old boy, Papa. The way he'd talk about the Black Noons and sage and the gazelle and the bustard and all those camel-mounted soldiers, shuffling along in a freezing night with the animals gurgling

68

	and moaning and the men in their Section messes . . . and singing . . .
FREDERICA:	We'll all be home soon.
ROBERT:	Except for Robin and the Brigadier.
WYATT:	Well, it's their home. And old Lamb's of course.
ALASTAIR:	And mine, God help me. Why I should be crimping in a place like this I'll never know.
ROBERT:	(*To* JED) What about you?
JED:	Any place is home for me. So who cares?
	(LEROI *enters with* MRS. JAMES.)
LEROI:	Mrs. James is here to see Mr. Gillman.
WYATT:	(*shouting off*) Christopher! (*To* MRS. JAMES) How nice of you to come and see me.
MRS. JAMES:	Not at all. It's quite an honour. I was told you wouldn't give interviews.
	(CHRISTOPHER *appears.*)
WYATT:	This is Mrs. James, Christopher. She's come to have a chat.
FREDERICA:	Do you want us to all go?
WYATT:	Not at all. I shan't feel half as self-conscious if I've got my chums around me.
CHRISTOPHER:	Do sit down, Mrs. James. Thank you, Leroi.
WYATT:	How very nice to meet you.
MRS. JAMES:	I hope it will be.
CHRISTOPHER:	Shall we start off right away? Or can I get you a drink or something?
MRS. JAMES:	No, thank you.
CHRISTOPHER:	Only he gets a little fatigued in this heat.
MRS. JAMES:	So do we all. I shan't take much of your time. If you've no objection, I'll just turn on this little tape-recorder. I hope it works all right.
CHRISTOPHER:	They all say that.
MRS. JAMES:	Do they? Well, I'll try and get it working. Could you just say a few words for level?
WYATT:	Who, me?

69

MRS. JAMES:	It is you I've come to interview.
WYATT:	Right. What about politics? Well, I'm just an old radical who detests progress. But then nobody hates it more. Don't you think, Mrs. James?
MRS. JAMES:	You're the one being interviewed. I'll just play that back.
	(*She does so.*)
MRS. JAMES:	That's fine.
WYATT:	Well, where shall we begin?
MRS. JAMES:	Wherever you like.
CHRISTOPHER:	You're the one conducting the interview.
WYATT:	I don't really know why you should want to talk to me at all. I've got no interesting views or opinions about anything. Never have done. I don't believe in much, never have done, never been inspired by anything. I'm simply over-talkative, vain, corpulent, and a bit of a played-out hulk, as I think most of the world knows and I'm surprised the news hasn't even reached this delightful little island of yours.
MRS. JAMES:	Isn't it a bit early to start being patronizing?
WYATT:	I am never patronizing. I am in no position to be so. And never have been.
MRS. JAMES:	How do you feel at the moment? How do you feel at the moment?
WYATT:	Just about the same as usual. Except hotter. Always weary, ineffably bored, always in some sort of vague pain and always with a bit of un-satisfying hatred burning away in the old inside like a heartburn or indigestion.
MRS. JAMES:	I can see we may not get very far.
WYATT:	Does it matter?
MRS. JAMES:	Not to you. I've simply been sent to do a job. Well, let's take an easy one first: what do you think of your fellow writers?

WYATT:	Fellow writers! What a dreadful expression!
MRS. JAMES:	I'm sorry, I couldn't think of anything else to describe the people who practise the same profession.
WYATT:	I try not to think of my fellow writers. If they're better than I am, I am disturbed. If they're worse, which is unusual, I simply feel sorry.
MRS. JAMES:	What do you think about the state of English literature at the moment?
WYATT:	Nothing at all.
MRS. JAMES:	Would you say that you strike postures with people whom you regard as provincials?
WYATT:	Very likely, I'm afraid. But not in your case. You're quite clearly very sophisticated. I mean, you wouldn't have much trouble getting the edge on me. You can never win an interview if you are being interviewed.
MRS. JAMES:	I'm not trying to win anything. I'm simply trying to arrive at some sort of approximation of the truth.
WYATT:	Do you think there is such a thing?
MRS. JAMES:	I don't think you should ask me facile questions, even if you are a famous man and paying us a visit.
WYATT:	I'm not paying you a visit. I am visiting my daughter and her husband. And staying with my other daughters and friends.
MRS. JAMES:	Do you think we should give up this interview?
WYATT:	I think that onus is entirely upon you.
MRS. JAMES:	Quite right. What do you think of as being Utopia?
WYATT:	A place without pain, passion or nobility. Where there is no hatred, boredom or imperfection.
MRS. JAMES:	What do you think of man?
WYATT:	As a defect, striving for excellence.

MRS. JAMES:	Do you really think that?
WYATT:	No, but presumably you want me to say something, however dull. However, I do think that there is a disastrously false, and very modern, idea that you can be absolutely honest.
MRS. JAMES:	How do you feel about your present work?
WYATT:	At the moment I don't really have any present work to speak of.
MRS. JAMES:	But has any of it been an advance?
WYATT:	The idea of advance is only something that is nurtured by uncreative people and critics.
MRS. JAMES:	You are well known for being over-sensitive to criticism.
WYATT:	Am I? I simply dislike it like a dog dislikes fleas.
MRS. JAMES:	Didn't Doctor Johnson say that?
WYATT:	Probably, but I should have thought the old boy would have put it a bit better, don't you?
MRS. JAMES:	Do you deliberately adopt a public pose?
WYATT:	Yes.
MRS. JAMES:	Why?
WYATT:	Because it makes life slightly more tolerable. The same applies to private life.
MRS. JAMES:	Then why do you consent to be interviewed?
WYATT:	I need the money.
MRS. JAMES:	But we can't afford to pay you.
WYATT:	I'm afraid Christopher didn't tell me that.
MRS. JAMES:	What do you think about religion today?
WYATT:	I think about religion if I think about it at all as it was in any time in human history. I think about it as the exercise of law as applied by each man to himself, even if that law be anarchy, negation or despair. If you're really interested, and it's pretty clear that you can't be interested in a pontificating old English buffer like me, that I also believe in what St. Augustine called "the

72

harsh necessity of sin". It's a ponderous phrase but probably no worse than "make love not war" and of course, I've always been very keen on the King James Bible and the English genius to boot, which it is being booted very swiftly, oh and good old Cranmer's Book of Common Prayer. It's like the Bible, it combines profundity without complexity.

MRS. JAMES: What do you think about protest movements?

WYATT: Protest is easy. But grief must be lived. As dear old Yeats said, dear old thing, be *secret* and *exult*. Secret . . .

MRS. JAMES: Would you say that you are a neurotic?

WYATT: On the whole, yes, all neurotics are bullies. But then so are most interviewers.

MRS. JAMES: Going back again to one of your favourite topics, critics . . .

WYATT: One of yours too, so it seems.

MRS. JAMES: What would you say was the function of critics, if any?

WYATT: Critics are sacrosanct. You must make it clear to your readers that they are simply and obviously more important than poets or writers. That's why you should always get in with them. You see, what we chaps do may be all right in its little way but what really counts is the fact that if it weren't for the existence of critics, we shouldn't be around at all or would just be on the dole or running chicken farms. Never make cheap jokes about critics. You've got to remember this: the critic is above criticism because he has the good sense never to do anything. He's up there helping us poor little guys to understand what the hell we're doing, which is a jolly helpful thing, you must agree. And if he stops you from writing at all then he's done the best job possible. After all, who wants to read or listen to what some poor old writer has pumped out of his diseased heart when he can read a balanced and reasoned judgement about life, love and literature from an aloof and informed commentator.

MRS. JAMES: Now that you have reached a certain stage in life, what, in fact, do you think about things like being in love?

WYATT: I think: thank God I don't have to be in love any more.

MRS. JAMES: What do you think you are?

WYATT: I think I'm probably what my daughter Frederica says she is, just a lot of hot shit, if you'll pardon the expression, blood, vanity and a certain prowess.

MRS. JAMES: There is a rumour that you have given up writing altogether.

WYATT: Heard that did you? Hear that, Christopher? God, that was the rumour I tried to spread about myself.

MRS. JAMES: In these changing times, do you still believe that words in themselves have any meaning, value or validity?

WYATT: I still cling pathetically to the old bardic belief that "words alone are certain good".

MRS. JAMES: Do you still live in London for any reason?

WYATT: Same reason as dear old Yeats again. Lived in Dublin. Great hatred. Little room.

MRS. JAMES: Do you see art as going in any particular direction now?

WYATT: I can hardly see the table in front of me. All art is simply criticism now. Posturing as art, self-evaluating, categorizing, constitutional, branded, hectoring and elbowing everyone out of the way.

MRS. JAMES: What do you think about friendship?

74

WYATT: A lost art. You should be able to discuss your friend's colds or toothaches as if they were railway disasters. As long as you both know they're not.

MRS. JAMES: Now, to a difficult question, as I know you have not been here long. What are your feelings about the island and the people you've met?

WYATT: All the good things I've seen of the island seem to be legacies of the British, the Spanish and the Dutch, particularly in the buildings and what's left of any proper dispensation of the law. As for the people, they seem to me to be a very unappealing mixture of hysteria and lethargy, brutality and sentimentality.

MRS. JAMES: Would you like me to turn this thing off?

WYATT: Not for my sake. I'm past protection. Aren't I, Christopher?

MRS. JAMES: Women have figured a great deal in your life.

WYATT: That sounds like a criticism veiled as a question.

MRS. JAMES: What would you say your feelings are about women nowadays?

WYATT: I have very little to do with women nowadays. As you can see, I've never been particularly attractive and if you want to ask that sort of question, and you clearly do, I'm pretty well past it anyway. The trouble with women is that I've always made a cardinal mistake: of treating them as friends and equals which they patently are not. Women only really love bullies.

MRS. JAMES: Don't you think that's a sweeping statement?

WYATT: Yes.

MRS. JAMES: What do you think about the class situation in England?

WYATT: I'm very fond of it. It provides a great deal of entertainment, fun and speculation for people who have nothing better to do. Like many of the

75

	upper class, I've liked the sound of broken glass.
MRS. JAMES:	What about God?
WYATT:	I say, we are getting down to it, aren't we? Are you sure you won't have a drink? I've always had a bit of a leaning towards him. I think perhaps people nowadays, people probably make the mistake of thinking of God as some sort of competitive family concern. You know, who might be pushed out of the market by a bit of smart operation.
MRS. JAMES:	You seem to keep referring to boredom. Is it an obsession with you?
WYATT:	No, I'm a bit too keen on myself. But I think everyone should have a daily ration of it.
MRS. JAMES:	Going back to literature——
WYATT:	Oh, is it still there?
MRS. JAMES:	Do you believe in the New Testament idea of the Gift of Tongues?
WYATT:	Yes I do. Mine was just a rather flabby, flailing thing. Everyone said I was rhetorical rather than recondite. And I think they were right.
MRS. JAMES:	How would you describe yourself politically?
WYATT:	I wouldn't attempt to. For one thing it isn't interesting enough. I believe in work but not in work to keep out all this desolation we live in. I believe in charity and I don't mean in the American sense, which is having buddies so that you can get on. I don't think I really believe in going on strike, even when some poor devil's in the right. My father believed that. Do you know one thing I'm really ashamed of? I drove a bus in the general strike. I thought I was such a dashing fellow.
MRS. JAMES:	Everyone always thinks of you as a very English writer——

WYATT: Oh, do they really?

MRS. JAMES: You know perfectly well. Do you think that there is still something special about being English rather than some other nationality?

WYATT: I don't know. I always think that there's something like a certain form of, say, cloud formation, called the English imagination. And if ever there was a critic's phrase, I think that's probably one.

MRS. JAMES: Do you think of yourself as an artist?

WYATT: Everyone nowadays is apparently an artist.

MRS. JAMES: But do you believe it?

WYATT: No. I believe in special gifts. Just as I believe some people are better than others.

MRS. JAMES: Do you believe in the family?

WYATT: I don't believe in its continuance, if that's what you mean. I do think it had its pleasures while it lasted and I was fortunate enough to have enjoyed and suffered them. I had a father whom I loved and now I have daughters whom I love, no doubt largely selfishly. But I wouldn't call it a write-off either for them or me. Or indeed their mother. Like the passing of empires and pride of tongue.

MRS. JAMES: Do you think that the relation between the sexes is healthier now than when you were a young man?

WYATT: Yes. But less pleasurable and less enduring. But that is not a question to ask an old man.

MRS. JAMES: What do you think of young people?

WYATT: I try not to. But then I've always preferred the instinct of friendship to that of the herd.

MRS. JAMES: What do you think of as real sin?

WYATT: The incapacity for proper despair. About talking about loss of faith as if it were some briefcase you've left behind you on the tube.

MRS. JAMES: What do you look on as virtue then?

77

WYATT:	True innocence.
MRS. JAMES:	Lastly, Mr. Gillman, what do you dread most at this stage of your life?
WYATT:	Not death. But ludicrous death. And I also feel it in the air. (*Long pause. Enter* TWO AMERICAN TOURISTS. *They are* MR. *and* MRS. DEKKER.)
FREDERICA:	Yes?
MRS. DEKKER:	Oh, we were just looking for the gift shop.
FREDERICA:	Well, I'm afraid this isn't the gift shop.
MRS. DEKKER:	Oh, dear, I'm so sorry. It's just that my husband and I, Mr. Dekker here, wanted to buy a few things to take back home. We've bought something from every place we've been.
FREDERICA:	I think the place you're looking for is just down the road.
MRS. DEKKER:	Oh dear, I'm so sorry. This must be a private home.
FREDERICA:	That was what my sister hoped.
MRS. DEKKER:	Only you see Mr. Dekker and I are on this cruise and they told us the gift shop was just down the road.
FREDERICA:	Well, it is. But I'm afraid we've nothing to sell.
MRS. DEKKER:	We're with the Folk Song and Dance Society of America.
ALASTAIR:	How nice for you. You all have such lovely hair.
MRS. DEKKER:	Do you live here? You actually live here?
FREDERICA:	My sister and her husband live here and so do two of these gentlemen. The rest of us are what is known as "passing through".
MR. DEKKER:	Having intruded upon you in this way, may I ask you a small favour?
BRIGADIER:	Certainly.
MR. DEKKER:	May we take a photograph of your beautiful home?
BRIGADIER:	By all means. Garden as well if you like.

MRS. DEKKER:	And could we take a picture of you all as well?
FREDERICA:	Why not go the whole hog?
MRS. DEKKER:	My husband, Mr. Dekker, just loves to take momentos.
FREDERICA:	Yes, they are nice, aren't they?
	(*They all pose quickly while* MR. DEKKER *takes his photographs*.)
MRS. DEKKER:	Well, thank you all so much. It was a real pleasure meeting you all.
FREDERICA:	Likewise, Mrs. Dekker.
	(MR. *and* MRS. DEKKER *wave farewell and go out*.)
	(*Pause*.)
HARRY:	(*To* FREDERICA) You didn't have to be like that, you know. They're harmless.
FREDERICA:	You think so?
HARRY:	I know so.
FREDERICA:	Why do you really live here? Is it really just because you want to bring water down from the mountains to a lot of people who aren't that bothered anyway?
WYATT:	I thought they were a nice couple of old dears.
FREDERICA:	No, you didn't. You pretend that you did. Like you've pretended to so much else always.
ROBIN:	Frederica—leave Father alone.
FREDERICA:	Why should I? (*To* WYATT) The trouble with you is that you've always been allowed to get away with it. Yes, I mean, get away with it. Like some of us can't. You get away with it all. Bad manners. Laziness. Cowardice. Lateness. Hurtful indiscretion. And we're all supposed to be stunned by the humour and eccentricity of it.
	(*Pause*.)
WYATT:	I *am* a clown. . . . People laugh at me in the street when they see me. But, as you say, it's my own fault.

(WYATT *gets to his feet.*)
Think I need a bit of a walk after that lunch with the Brigadier.
(*They all watch him go off in the direction of the beach.*)

CURTAIN

END OF ACT TWO, SCENE ONE

ACT TWO, SCENE TWO

The same evening, as before. The air seems still and there is a strange noise of resentful-sounding music in the distance. Dogs howl. FREDERICA *picks up a cushion dropped by* LEROI. *She goes for a cigarette and, having got it, turns and almost bumps into* CHRISTOPHER.

FREDERICA: Edward's talked to that boy down on that beach nearly all day long. Why can't *he* shut him up! Or Robin! She's supposed to be such a hostess. Any of you. You. You're Wyatt's Great Protector . . . Aren't you? But, no, you all let the boy just go on and on—and Daddy pretending to be deaf . . . all the while. Don't bother to answer . . .

CHRISTOPHER: I won't. Even if I could.
(*She offers him a cigarette.*)
Strange sound . . .

FREDERICA: What?

CHRISTOPHER: The music.

FREDERICA: Not very attractive. I suppose they think it has a simple, brooding native charm and vitality. Which is about the last thing any of them have got. Anyway, they never stop playing it.

CHRISTOPHER: Tourists like it, I suppose.

FREDERICA: They would. . . . Why did you leave your wife and give up everything for the old man? It can't be much fun. Or is it?

CHRISTOPHER: You do ask direct questions, don't you?

FREDERICA: Only when I think I might get a direct answer. Rather charmless really.

CHRISTOPHER: Well . . .

FREDERICA: No. You needn't tell me if you don't want. Or fictionalize just to please me.

CHRISTOPHER: I want to please you.

FREDERICA: Please *me*? Why?

CHRISTOPHER: Because, well, I've simply got a thing, this thing about you. For you.

FREDERICA: Why?

CHRISTOPHER: Oh, lots of reasons. You're in pain a lot of the time.

FREDERICA: I don't need a nurse, thanks. Anyway, you've got the old man and he needs ten blooming nursemaids and God knows what.

CHRISTOPHER: No. I didn't fancy my chances.

FREDERICA: Right. There's no future in me. Not for anyone. One day it'll be just . . . *out*. . . . Tell me about your wife.

CHRISTOPHER: She just, didn't fancy me, that's all.

FREDERICA: Perhaps you weren't very fanciable.

CHRISTOPHER: Indeed. So I left her the house, most of the money . . . and the child . . . I minded that . . .

FREDERICA: The child?

CHRISTOPHER: Yes.

FREDERICA: I wonder if you really did. Or was it the house and the money? Is the old boy a fair exchange?

CHRISTOPHER: I think so . . . I admire him.

FREDERICA: Do you?

CHRISTOPHER: Do you think I'm bent?

FREDERICA: No. Just a bit potty. Like most of us . . .

CHRISTOPHER: There was another woman who didn't fancy me either. So I just gave up.

FREDERICA: Faint of heart.

CHRISTOPHER: Quite.

FREDERICA: You're quite attractive.

CHRISTOPHER: Not very. . . . You know that boy Jed. He reminds me of a young S.S. man I killed in the war. Unarmed prisoner. A G.I. tried to stop me so I shot him too.

FREDERICA: Now, that's *not* attractive.

CHRISTOPHER: No. . . . Not a bit . . .

FREDERICA: Did you get away with it?

CHRISTOPHER: Oh, yes. It's amazing what you can.

FREDERICA: Don't we all know? . . . Why does he pretend to be deaf and in front of Jed?

(*Pause.*)

(*The rest of the company come in from the dining-room. They all look uneasy, particularly* ALASTAIR, *who is hysterical.*)

ALASTAIR: (*To everyone*) I told him to go! I told him to go! But he won't! He just won't! Oh God!

(ALASTAIR *sits down and weeps silently.*)

Just another of my crying jags . . .

(JED *looks down at* ALASTAIR *contemptuously and then turns to address everyone else.*)

JED: You all, you all bastards . . . I sit here listening to you. Having your fancy dinner and your wine from France and England. You know what I think of you? What *we* think of you? What we think of you? Fuck all your *shit*—that's what we think. One person, not like any one of you here, even if he's the God-damnest cretin, I'd make him God, yes, man, rather than you. You hear? Hear me. Listen to me if you can hear anything but the sound of your own selves and present. I'm not interested in your arguments, not that they are, of your so-called memories and all that pathetic shit. The only thing that matters, man, is blood, man. Blood. . . . You know what that means? No, no, you surely as to hell don't. No, no when you pigs, you pigs go, it ain't going to be no fucking fourth of July. All I see, and I laugh when I see it, man, I laugh, is you pigs barbecued, barbecued in your own shit. *We're*, yes, we're going to take over and don't you begin to forget it. Man, I feel real sorry for you lot. No, I don't. . . . You got it coming. And you *have soon*. Think of the theatre of the mind, baby, old moulding babies, except you won't. We count and we *do*, not like you, we *really*, really do. . . . Why, we fall about laughing at you people, not people, you're not people, you pigs. We are people. *We* are. But not you. You don't understand and why should you because, believe me, babies, old failing babies, words, yes I mean words, even what I'm saying to you now, is going to be the first to go. Go, baby. Go. You can't even make love. Do you understand one word, those old words you love so much, what I mean? No. And you won't. If it ain't written down, you don't believe it. . . . There's only one word left and you know what that is. It's fuck, man. Fuck. . . . That's the last of the English for you babies. Or maybe shit. Because that's what we're going to do on you. Shit. That's what you'll all go down in. One blissful, God-like shit. *You*

83

think we're mother-fucking, stinking, yelling, shouting shits. Well that's what we are, babies. And there's nothing, not nothing you or anybody else can do about it. Jesus is sort of shit. But you're not even *shit*. We think, we fuck and we shit and that's what we do and you're on the great gasping end of it. Because you're pigs. Just take one little look at yourselves. You're pigs, babies. Pigs. And we're gonna shit you out of this world, babies. Right out of this mother-fucking world. You know what? I just had an idea. Like that old prick writer there. Colonialism is the fornication of the twentieth century. You can't be young. . . . So all you'd better do, all you *will* do, is die, die, baby. And pretty soon. Just real soon. Like tomorrow. Or even tonight.

(*There is a short pause.*)

CHRISTOPHER: I remember killing someone like you. Only he was blond.

JED: Yes? Well, just remember it. Because you may not remember it much longer.

(*Pause.*)

WYATT: I was never a *young* man. I think I always felt old. I was always wrinkled somehow. More than I am now. Well, nearly. Now I am sort of old. No, old. But something always kept telling me I was young. Very young. But, of course, I never was. Something started without me. Too slow. Never got off the old ground. Never got off the ground. Wasn't sure about the ground at all. Never capable of inspecting it. Or, anyway, closely. Not closely. . . . Not closely. . . . I think I ought to go to bed.

(*As* WYATT *rises to go, several armed islanders appear out of the darkness. He looks at them with*

their firearms pointing at the group and turns to
run away. They shoot him down.)
(*Pause.*)

EDWARD: There's an old English saying. Don't suppose
you'd know it . . .

JED: So? What is it?

EDWARD: My God—they've shot the fox . . .

CURTAIN

END OF PLAY